W9-BRI-545

Israel

Israel

BY MARTIN HINTZ
AND STEPHEN HINTZ

Enchantment of the World
Second Series

Children's Press®

A Division of Grolier Publishing

NEW YORK   LONDON   HONG KONG   SYDNEY
DANBURY, CONNECTICUT

Consultant: Esther Raizen, Ph.D., Assistant Professor and Hebrew Language
Coordinator, The University of Texas at Austin

Please note: All statistics are as up-to-date as possible at the time of publication.

Visit Children's Press on the Internet: http://publishing.grolier.com

Book production: Herman Adler Design Group

Library of Congress Cataloging-in-Publication Data

Hintz, Martin.
    Israel / by Martin Hintz and Stephen Hintz.
      p. cm. — (Enchantment of the world. Second series)
    Includes bibliographical references and index.
    Summary: Describes the geography, plants and animals, history,
economy, language, religions, culture, and people of Israel, a young
nation celebrating its fiftieth birthday in 1998.
    ISBN 0-516-21108-0
    1. Israel—Juvenile literature. [1. Israel.] I. Hintz, Stephen V.
II. Title. III. Series.
DS126.5.H529 1999
915.694—dc21   98-17642
                                                       CIP
                                                        AC

GROLIER
PUBLISHING

Acknowledgments

For their assistance behind the scenes, as well as their suggestions, tips, and hospitality, the authors wish to thank Aire Sommer, Ministry of Tourism commissioner for North America; Geoffrey Weill and his staff at Geoffrey Weill & Associates; Barbara Sharon Bahny and Tsion Ben David, both of the Israel Ministry of Tourism; Martin Davidson, branch manager, hosting operations division, Israel Ministry of Tourism; guide Jeff Abel, who translated his knowledge into easily understood terms; Rachel Grodjinovsky, director of foreign affairs, Suzanne Dellal Centre for Dance and Theatre; Katrin Lieberwirth, Hyatt International; publisher Asher Weill, *Ariel* magazine; Sandy Barkin, director of public affairs, Supreme Court of Israel; Nachman Klieman and Sheryl Stein, El Al Israel Airlines; Varda Chassel, marketing director, Kibbutz Hotels Chain; and Charles Croce, director of corporate communications— The Americas, Lufthansa German Airlines.

Thanks also to Gil Goldfine, Goldfine & Partners; Janet Inbar, director of international relations, Tel Aviv Museum of Art; Tom Huntington, editor, *Historical Traveler*; Ali Halabi, Daliat el Carmel local council tourism representative; and the many other friends who made our visits to Israel so productive and valuable: Nabeel Naser El-deen, Yona Kalimovitzki, Barbara Liebgott, and Jacob Sudri; and Judean Desert guide Ofer Netzer, who can drive his truck straight up the Judean Desert cliffsides. Special accolades to Weiss Topographers and to Angela Callies-Jacobs.

Contents

CHAPTER

ONE   A Land of Milk and Honey 8

TWO   Spotlight on the Landscape 14

THREE   Israel's Wilder Side 24

FOUR   From the Ancients to Today 32

FIVE   Birth and Growth of a Nation 50

SIX   The Business of Business Is Business 62

SEVEN   A People Potpourri 76

EIGHT   A Colorful Religious Mosaic 88

NINE   Arts and Sports across Ethnic Lines 104

TEN   The Cousins Are Coming 118

Cover photo:
Jerusalem

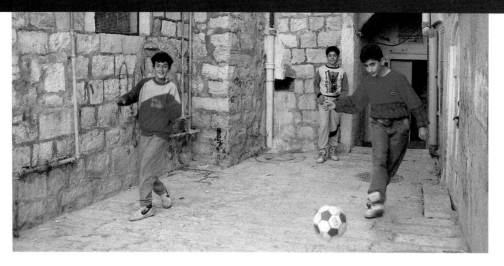

Soccer practice

Timeline.....................**128**

Fast Facts....................**130**

To Find Out More...........**134**

Index........................**136**

Jewish children

CHAPTER

ONE

A Land of Milk and Honey

Israel—where ancient ways meet today's world. Israel—a biblical land flowing with milk and honey. Israel—where prophets walked.

8

THE DESERT SHIMMERS UNDER A BLAZING SUN. IN THE distance, a long line of camels slowly pick their way across the sand- and rock-strewn hills. Hanging tightly to their saddles, Bedouin riders bend into the heat. They seem to move across a vast lake, but the lake is only a mirage.

This could be a parched country, but natural springs and deep wells support swaths of vegetation amid the dull golden rocks. Irrigated green fields dazzle the eye, while ranks of towering date palms stand guard against the encroaching sand. Modern cities and suburban settlements tiptoe across a once-barren landscape, spreading out across the desert in growth fueled by piped-in water.

Israel's cities are a wonderful mix of the very old and the very new. Pilgrims of many faiths flock to Jerusalem. The golden exterior of the Dome of the Rock glows in the sunset. This is the mosque where the Muslim prophet Muhammad is said to have ascended into Paradise. At the "Wailing Wall," the remnants of the Western Wall of the Second Temple, Jews touch their past by running their fingers along the cold stones.

Opposite: **Irrigated fields in Galilee, seen from Mount Tabor**

The Dome of the Rock, in Jerusalem

A Land of Milk and Honey **9**

Geopolitical map of Israel

ISRAEL
- Cities of over 50,000 people
- Smaller cities and towns

0   20 miles
0   30 kilometers

LEBANON

SYRIA

MEDITERRANEAN SEA

GOLAN HEIGHTS

Meiron Golan

▲ Har Meron 3,963 ft. (1,208 m)

Nahariyya
'Akko (Acre)
Qiryat Yam
Haifa
Dalyat al-Karmel
Ein Hod
Zikhron Ya'aqov

Zefat   Rosh Pinna
Galilee
Teverya (Tiberius)   *Yam Kinneret (Sea of Galilee)*
Zippori
Nazareth   Degania
NORTHERN   Yarmuk

HAIFA
Hadera

Giv'at Hayyim
Netanya
TEL AVIV   *CENTRAL*
Ramat Gan
Tel Aviv-Jaffa   Petah Tiqwa
Bat Yam   Kefar Sava
Holon   Ramia
Lod (Lydda)   Rehovot
Ashdod
JERUSALEM

WEST BANK
Nablus
Samaria
Jordan
Zarqa

EL GHOR

SYRIAN DESERT

Jerusalem ✪
Jericho
Khirbet Qumran
Bethlehem

★ Amman

JORDAN

Ashqelon
Qiryat Gat   Hebron
Gaza
GAZA STRIP
Khan Yunis

Beersheba
(Be'er Sheva')

Dead Sea
Mojib

ISRAEL

SOUTHERN

Besor

NEGEV DESERT

EL GHOR

Araba

Occupied Areas:
Golan Heights: annexed 1981
West Bank: occupied since 1967
Gaza Strip: occupied since 1967

EGYPT

SINAI DESERT

ARAVA DESERT

N
W   E
S

Eilat

ISRAEL

Not far away are the holiest shrines of Christianity. Vendors in the ancient city peer out from their stalls, ready to bargain with customers.

The Western Wall

On the coast, modern Tel Aviv bustles alongside the ancient port of Jaffa. Tel Aviv's sidewalk cafés, towering office buildings, world-famous opera, trendy art museums,

Tel Aviv's skyline, from Jaffa

wide parkways, and fast-moving traffic mark it as a city on the move. The fortresslike United States Embassy is only a block from the gray-green waters of the Mediterranean Sea. Along with other diplomatic missions in the city, the U.S. Embassy helps ensure that the eyes of the world remain on Israel. Schoolchildren dash through the streets of Tel Aviv, chattering like magpies.

In the now-fertile countryside, the swish-swish of water spraying from irrigation hoses is an agricultural symphony. Plump, ripe tomatoes wait to be picked. The fronds of date palms dance in the breeze.

Irrigating their spirit, Christian pilgrims from around the world are baptized in the River Jordan. Their white robes billow in the muddy waters.

Not far away, fishers cast their nets across the calm waters of Yam Kinneret, the Sea of Galilee. The only visible difference between today and a thousand years ago is the outboard motor sported by each small boat. The region was settled long ago by the Romans as the resort of Tiberias. To the east, the Golan Heights overlook the peaceful scene. Now occupied by Israeli settlers, the heights were once battlegrounds between Arabs and Israelis.

Fishing on the Sea of Galilee

Near Solomon's Pools, south of Jerusalem and Bethlehem on the road to Hebron, shepherd boys scramble their long-eared donkeys up and over the low ridges. They follow flocks of black and white sheep grazing on the scrub grasses. At the Canada Centre, a Canadian-built sports center in Metulla near the Lebanese border far to the north, other kids play ice hockey.

Now move on to more images: newspaper photos of stone-throwing, screaming crowds; gun-toting soldiers with serious faces; and in the vast assembly hall of the United Nations (UN), arguments over the meaning of peace. Next, shift to dusty Bethlehem, where Jesus Christ is said to have been born. The shrine built over his humble birthplace, the Grotto of the

Bethlehem has many Christian churches.

Nativity, is perfumed with incense. Standing outside, an armed Palestinian police officer smiles at the crowds. Turn back to magazine layouts of shawl-clad Jews praying; then click on to a television portrait of an Arab *muezzin* (a Muslim crier) calling the faithful to prayer.

All this is Israel, a young nation that celebrated its fiftieth birthday in 1998. Yet Israel is more than simply a country. Israel is also a spiritual landscape. It is a state of mind, an emotion, and a melting pot of contrasting dreams. It is a state of enthusiasm, optimism, concern, and faith.

Israel is an intricate social web of religion and politics, of tradition and today's reality, of military preparedness and economic muscle. To understand it all can be difficult. Let's try.

Spotlight on the Landscape

Israel is easy to find. Put a finger on a map of the world. Find the Mediterranean Sea, an expanse of water south of Europe. Run your finger straight east until you reach the closest beach. That's Israel.

This wedge-shaped country borders the Mediterranean Sea, with Egypt to the southwest, Lebanon to the north, Jordan to the east, and Syria to the northeast. In the 1990s, Israel's territory was in a state of constant change. The land the country controlled was changing as the political situation in the region evolved and talks continued between the Israelis and their Arab neighbors. In 1998, the country's landscape totaled 8,474 square miles (21,946 sq km). This included the Golan Heights and East Jerusalem. Israel is only a shade larger than the state of New Jersey. About 21 percent of the land is arable, or suitable for farming, and this percentage is continually growing.

Opposite: **A boat harbor in Eilat, on the Gulf of Aqaba**

Israel has a long border on the Mediterranean Sea.

Borders Change

Determining Israel's exact acreage at any one time is difficult. The country's borders are ever-changing as international politics wrestle with who actually controls its various parts. As of 1998, Israel's borders ran for 625 miles (1,006 km), not including the coastline. Of this, 158 miles (255 km) bordered Egypt; 32 miles (51 km) stretched along the Gaza Strip; 148 miles (238 km) ran along Jordan; 49 miles (79 km) bordered

Geographical Features

Highest Elevation: Mount Meron *(Har Meron)*, 3,963 feet (1,208 m)

Lowest Elevation: Dead Sea, 1,312 feet (400 m) below sea level

Longest River: Jordan River, 200 miles (322 km)

Widest Lake: Sea of Galilee, 64 square miles (166 square km)

Largest City: Jerusalem, 602,100 residents (1996; includes East Jerusalem)

Highest Average Temperature: 100°F (38°C) along the Dead Sea

Lowest Average Temperature: 50°F (10°C)

Lebanon; 47 miles (76 km) ran along Syria in the Golan Heights area; and 191 miles (307 km) were on the West Bank. The Gaza Strip, which borders Egypt and the Mediterranean Sea, and the West Bank, which borders Jordan, have been

occupied by Israel since 1967. Israel's scenic coastline meanders along cliffs and sandy beaches for 170 miles (273 km).

Negotiations are continuing between Israel and the Palestinian Authority, Syria, and Jordan to determine the final status of the land. Treaties have resolved some of the border questions.

The Gaza Strip is a 139-square-mile (360-sq-km) area of sand and boulders that was not included as part of Israel in the Israel-Egypt peace treaty of 1949. The Gaza Strip has been the home of Palestinian refugees who fled from Palestine when the state of Israel was formed. The area was under Egyptian and UN control over the years and is now managed by the Palestinians.

A young Palestinian refugee in the Gaza Strip

Jericho and its surrounding neighborhood, which had been part of Israel since 1967, came under Palestinian control in the mid-1990s. The transaction was due to an agreement between Israel and the Palestine Liberation Organization, a military-political group that has long been fighting for Palestinian territorial rights.

In 1994, the Israelis withdrew from the Gaza Strip, and by 1996, they had pulled out of most cities and towns along the West Bank of the Jordan.

The areas then came under Palestinian control. During the 1990s, however, many Israelis opposed the withdrawals.

Land Claimed

Israel has claimed large areas of the West Bank of the Jordan River and the entire city of Jerusalem. The Palestinians who live there also want stretches along the river and part of Jerusalem. They would claim the city as the capital of any future state of Palestine. Israel, however, views the whole of

New construction on the West Bank of the Jordan River

Jerusalem as its capital. A large portion of the population opposes the surrender of territories that were historically Jewish, such as Judea and Samaria. An ongoing, evolving peace process between Palestinians and Israelis is attempting to reconcile all these claims.

Israel also occupies a 3-mile (5-km)-wide security zone in southern Lebanon. This keeps Israeli settlements in the north relatively safe from rocket and terrorist attacks launched from Lebanon.

Most Israelis live in three distinct sections of the northern and central parts of the country. The first section is the Coastal Plain on the west, which includes the cities of Haifa and

Tel Aviv. Next is the Valley Region to the east, with the Jordan River linking the Sea of Galilee *(Yam Kinneret)* and the Dead Sea *(Yam Hamelah)*. The third is the area of Israel that includes the Galilee, Samaria, and Judea. Jerusalem lies on rocky land in the Judean Hills. A fourth major region of the country is the sprawling Negev Desert.

Jerusalem is Israel's largest city.

A road winds through the arid Negev Desert.

Deserts in the South

The southern part of Israel consists of the sprawling Negev and Arava red-sand deserts. The Ramon Crater *(Makhtesh Ramon)*, in the center of the Negev, is the world's largest natural crater at 5 miles (8 km) wide, 23 miles (37 km) long, and 1,000 feet (305 m) deep. The crater was caused by erosion, although it looks like a moonscape

Looking at Israel's Cities

Tel Aviv, the second-largest city in Israel after Jerusalem, is also the nation's business center. In 1996, the population of Tel Aviv and Jaffa (Yafo) was 353,100. Tel Aviv's cultural attractions include the Golda Meir Center for the Performing Arts with its Opera House and the Tel Aviv Museum of Art. The promenade along the beach (below) is a favorite place for joggers and strollers. Tel Aviv is known as the "city that never stops" because of its nightclubs, coffeehouses, and discos. The city was founded in 1909, as one of the first Jewish urban centers in Palestine. Temperatures in January range from 48 to 63°F (9 to 17°C) and in August are from 72 to 85°F (22 to 29°C).

The ancient port of Haifa was founded 4,000 years ago. Today, 255,300 people live in this leading cultural and entertainment center, with its Haifa Municipal Theater,

Tikutin Art Museum, and a large soccer stadium. A ship that ferried illegal Jewish emigrants to Palestine after World War II (1939–1945) sits atop the Clandestine Immigration and Naval Museum. A Baha'i temple—the world headquarters of this faith—stands on a hillside overlooking the downtown section. Haifa's population is diverse, and the city is known for its tradition of harboring religious minorities. Average daily temperatures are 57°F (14°C) in January and 81°F (27°C) in August.

Beersheba (Be'er Sheva') began as a Bedouin camel market and is now a vacation site and one of Israel's largest cities, with a 1992 population of 128,400. The Ben-Gurion University of the Negev there, founded in 1969, was named after Israel's first prime minister. The Israel Air Force Museum and the weekly Bedouin market are other attractions. The city is the jumping-off point for exploring the Negev Desert. The daily temperature ranges from 68 to 73°F (20 to 23°C) in January and averages 95°F (35°C) in August.

Eilat, on the Red Sea on the Gulf of Aqaba, is a major resort community of 33,300 residents. Centuries ago, the Queen of Sheba is said to have visited King Solomon in Eilat. Today, divers enjoy exploring the offshore reefs. Average daily temperatures are 82°F (28°C) in January and 95°F (35°C) in August.

Zefat (Safed), at 3,200 feet (975 m) above sea level, is the city "closest to heaven"—the highest in Israel. Zefat is the birthplace of the kabala—the teachings of Jewish mysticism—and is one of the four holy cities of Judaism. The first book in Hebrew was printed here in 1578. Dozens of artists have studios and galleries in this city of 30,000. The temperature ranges from 56°F (13°C) in January to 88°F (31°C) in August.

hit by a meteor. The Negev Desert is bordered by the Mediterranean Sea, the Sinai Desert, the Moab Mountains, and the Judean Desert.

The Dead Sea is actually a lake, and it is not really dead. At least eleven types of bacteria are found in its waters, which are about nine times as salty as the ocean. No other forms of life, however, can survive here. It is fun to float in the Dead Sea because you are held up by the dense water.

It's easy to float on the Dead Sea.

The Dead Sea is slowly shrinking at the rate of several feet a year. This is partly due to evaporation and partly due to the diversion of irrigation water from the Jordan River, which feeds into the sea.

The clear, blue-green sea is 34.1 miles (55 km) long and 1.8 to 11 miles (3 to 18 km) wide. Its reported depth at the deepest point is 1,418 feet (432 m) and only about 35 feet (11 m) on the south. At 1,312 feet (400 m) below sea level, the Dead Sea is lower than any other inland sea on earth. Ears pop and motorists yawn from the pressure when descending the long stretch of highway to the Dead Sea from Jerusalem.

Wooden Vessel

A 110-passenger ship, *Lot's Wife*, putt-putts across the dense waters of the Dead Sea. The vessel is made of wood because metal cannot withstand the sea's high salt and mineral content.

In 1947, Muhammad Adh Dhib, a young Bedouin, herded his goats along the western shore of the Dead Sea, near Khirbet Qumran. He found a cave in the cliff-side. Inside the cave were clay jars, one of which contained scrolls made of parchment and wrapped in linen. Other scrolls were found later. The writings were Scripture texts and descriptions of daily life written in Hebrew and Aramaic 100 years before Jesus Christ was born. The scrolls are displayed at the Shrine of the Book in the Israel Museum in Jerusalem.

The ship is named for the woman who, according to Scripture, disobeyed an angel's order not to look back on the destruction of the cities of Sodom and Gomorrah. She was turned into a pillar of salt for her curiosity and disobedience. Bromine, magnesium, and potassium chloride (potash) are among the natural resources taken from the lake waters and used for industry. Health-care products are also made from the minerals.

Famous Waterway

The Jordan River is one of the most famous waterways in the world, although it is only 200 miles (322 km) long. It was often mentioned in the Bible and is noted for its religious significance. The Jordan rises in the mountains of southern Lebanon and Syria and flows south through Israel to the Dead Sea, sometimes forming part of the border with Jordan. It also feeds and drains the Sea of Galilee.

The steep-sided river valley, called the Jordan Rift Valley, is 2 to 15 miles (3 to 24 km) wide. Most of its course is below sea level. During the hot summers, when the temperature hits 100°F (38°C), the water narrows to a stream. Many Israelis enjoy white-water rafting in the few stretches of wild, rock-cluttered water. Dams on the lower Jordan provide hydroelectric power.

The Sea of Galilee is historically and religiously important. It is a small lake, only about 15 miles (24 km) long and 7 miles (11 km) wide, with a depth of 155 feet (47 m). Fish thrive in its cold waters. While the sea is usually calm, downdrafts of cold air off the nearby hills can cause violent storms. A Bible story tells of Christ walking on its raging surface, thereby quieting the storm.

Running the Jordan River

Ablaze with Wildflowers

The surrounding countryside is ablaze with cypress and colorful wildflowers in the rainy winter. Ruins of ancient Greek and Roman cities encircle the water. The region has been a popular getaway spot since the time of emperors and kings.

Most Israelis want to be sure that their country's economic growth is not haphazard, and that the fragile ecosystem is protected. The Negev Center for Regional Development studies land issues in the far south, issuing scientific studies on industrial development, the environment, the climate, and other topics.

Israel's Wilder Side

Although Israel is a small country, its range of climate and geographical features support diverse plant and animal life. Israel has more than 2,800 plant species—as well as 8 amphibian species, 80 kinds of reptiles, 380 kinds of birds, and 80 mammal species.

ISRAEL IS ONE OF THE FEW NATIONS IN THE WORLD WHERE it is against the law to pick wildflowers. Picking flowers was once a popular pastime, but some plants almost became extinct because they were so popular for table arrangements. Activist groups work hard to ensure that future generations of Israelis can also enjoy the country's forests, mountains, waterfalls, and beaches. Even the deserts are important. The Negev Center for Regional Development was established in 1993 to study and control the impact of encroaching civilization on the great southern desert.

The Ministry of Environment is responsible for monitoring Israel's air, water, and land to make certain the activities of a modern society do not damage the surroundings.

Opposite: **An ibex surveys his turf in Ein Gedi Nature Reserve.**

Remote Areas Remain

Even as Israel spreads out from its cities, a few remote areas remain where wild creatures can live in relative peace. The mountain gazelle leaps from ridge to ridge in the high mountains. Nubian ibex race across the plains. Agama lizards and chameleons scurry among the desert rocks. To protect threatened plant and animal species, the Israelis have established the Nature Reserve Authority, which over-

A ground agama lizard

sees 150 animal- and plant-friendly havens. One such site is the Hula Nature Reserve in Upper Galilee near the artists' colony of Zefat. There are also three *hai-bar* reserves in the country. *Hai-bar* means "wild life" in Hebrew. These preserves are located at Yotvata north of Eilat, Haifa, and the Golan Heights.

The Hai-Bar National Biblical Wildlife Reserve, the largest of these three, is established on 8,000 acres (3,238 hectares) of salt flats near the Jordanian border. The Negev Desert creeps around the edges of this oasis, home to creatures mentioned in the Scriptures. The purpose of this breeding center is to raise enough exotic creatures so they can be released into the wild.

Oryx Has Long Horns

One such animal is the white oryx, a large, fleet-footed African antelope with long straight horns that project backward. Popular with marksmen for centuries, the white oryx was almost hunted to extinction until Hai-Bar began raising

Ostriches were flown to Hai-Bar from Ethiopia by the Israeli Air Force.

them in its safe environment. On the reserve's wide savanna, or plain, Somali wild asses also run wild. With their striped legs, they resemble a cousin of the zebra. Brought to Hai-Bar from Iran, the asses were extinct in Israel for two thousand years.

Some animals arrived at Hai-Bar in unusual ways. Mesopotamian fallow deer were smuggled from Iran in the 1970s during a violent revolution in that country. Ostrich chicks were flown out of Ethiopia by the Israeli Air Force.

A fennec fox

Also roaming the reserve is the red, big-eared fennec fox. This furry little fellow is the tiniest member of the fox family. The swift, lanky southern wolf also calls the Hai-Bar Reserve its home. Scientist Reuven Epher tracks the wolves on his radio equipment. Some of the wolves have collars with electronic devices that send signals for Epher's machinery to record. Tracing the wolves' movement broadens knowledge of how these elusive animals live.

Zoological Gardens Open

The Tisch Family Biblical Zoo and Zoological Gardens in Jerusalem attracts Israelis of all ages. The zoo opened in 1993. At the entrance, a pond provides a habitat for waterfowl. Ducks, pelicans, swans, and cormorants paddle happily in the water. Instead of living in cages, the zoo's larger residents live behind glass windows or wide trenches that separate them from other species. Parrots caw, long-tailed monkeys chatter, and rare Asiatic lions roar, making an animal symphony.

Taking a break on a visit to the zoo in Jerusalem

A yellow-vented bulbul

The zoo's Syrian brown bears look as if they are ready to make a run for it. If they could, they can gallop at 25 miles (40 km) per hour! Youngsters can pet camels, ride ponies, and generally get close to the safer creatures.

Birds flock everywhere in Israel. The common bulbul, sylvia warblers, goldcrests, hawks, and falcons are full-time residents. The International Birdwatching Center near Eilat enables Israeli and foreign ornithologists (scientists who study birds) to study the hundreds of thousands of birds that live in the region. The birdwatchers are kept busy. They identify honey buzzards and other birds that annually migrate to and from Africa in March and October.

Bedouins Gather

Every Thursday, Bedouins gather at the sheep, goat, and camel market at Beersheba (Be'er Sheva'), the largest city in the Negev Desert, where buyers and sellers bargain. The open square is noisy and dusty and the cries of the various creatures

are deafening. When the livestock is sold, the money is some-times used to buy television sets and pickup trucks. This is one example of changes that affect the traditional way of life for some of the desert people.

The Bedouin market at Beersheba

Canaan dogs are well suited for herding animals.

City Is Jump-Off Point

Donkeys, horses, and camels are still regularly used in Israel. In 1948, the Beersheba market was almost the only going business in that city of a few thousand residents. Today, Israelis use the city as a jumping-off point for desert tours. They often hire Bedouins as guides.

Arab, Bedouin, and Druze shepherds use the sharp-eyed Canaan dog to round up their flocks. This tough breed dates

Prize of the Desert

The camel remains the most prized animal in the desert. Camels, like cattle, sheep, buffalo, giraffes, and llamas, are ruminants that chew a cud. A cud is a mouthful of previously swallowed food that has been brought back up to the mouth from one of the animal's several stomach chambers.

Camels have been domesticated for thousands of years. They are used for carrying heavy loads and for transporting people across desert land. Their meat is good to eat and their milk is delicious. In fact, camel's milk is the only kind of milk that does not curdle. A camel can store up to 1.5 gallons (5.7 l) of water, enough to last it for about three days. The camel's face is designed by nature to protect the animal in the harsh desert. Its long eyelashes keep out the blowing sand, and its eyelids and nose even funnel rainwater to its mouth. Fat is stored in the humps on its back.

The dromedary, or one-humped camel, is the most prevalent in the Middle East. It has short hair, long, skinny legs, and wide pads on its sensitive feet that enable it to cross sandy terrain. Camels are usually 6 to 7 feet (1.8 to 2.1 m) tall at the shoulder. They can trot for many hours at about 9 miles (14.5 km) per hour.

back to prebiblical days. It can trot for hours over the harsh landscape and can quickly change direction.

The Jewish National Fund was founded in 1901 to purchase land in the region. It also carried out forest-reclamation projects throughout Palestine. By independence in 1948, the fund had purchased 240,000 acres (97,000 ha) and planted

4.5 million trees on the boulder-strewn hillsides. By the late 1990s, more than 200 million trees had been planted, covering 300,000 acres (121,000 ha). Many of the trees are oak, once a major part of the biblical landscape. Carob, terbinth, cypress, eucalyptus, Judas, acacia, olive, pine, and almond trees are also planted.

Each winter, Israelis celebrate *Tu B'shvat.* This is the "New Year of Trees," a holiday of tree-planting. Israelis of all ages turn out for planting ceremonies. In biblical times, the festival was known as *Rosh Hashana la-Ilanot.*

A Jewish National Fund forest

Most cities have extensive gardens in their parks and along roads. The country's hot sun brings out the rich colors of flowers and bushes. To view native plants from various parts of the country, Israelis enjoy visiting the extensive gardens of Neot Kedumim, a landscape reserve in the center of Israel.

Planting trees near Jerusalem

From the Ancients to Today

As a modern nation, Israel is a youngster, having celebrated its 50th birthday in 1998. But the story of this nation spans more than five decades. The birth and growth of today's Israel is the latest chapter in a tale that spans thousands of years. Throughout the centuries, a race of devout people, the Jews, made an already ancient landscape part of their spirit. No matter where they lived, they could always look to their homeland.

ISRAEL'S STORY IS CLOSELY TIED TO THAT OF THE REST OF THE Middle East, which some historians call the "cradle of civilization." Between the fertile valley of Mesopotamia to the east and the Nile Valley in Egypt to the west was Palestine, the country's name during Roman times. Its geographic position made Palestine a crossroads for armies, refugees, nomads, and spiritual leaders.

Ancient Caves Found

Archaeologists have found evidence of humans living in caves before the founding of Jericho, a city that can trace its roots back 9,000 to 11,000 years. Flint tools and remains of woven mats

Country Names

Philistia was an ancient country in the region. The word *Philistine* is the root word for "Palestine." The Philistines were enemies of the early Israelites. The word *Israel* is the name given by God to the biblical character Jacob, one of the three fathers of the Hebrew nation. Jacob had twelve sons, whose offspring were grouped into the Twelve Tribes of Israel.

Excavations at Jericho show human settlements dating from about 8000 B.C.

Opposite: **The Tower of David Citadel in Jerusalem**

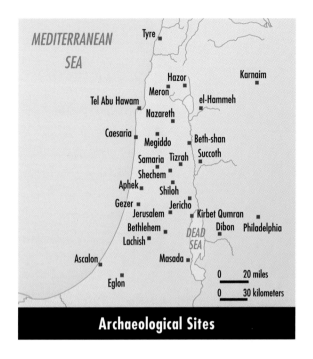

MEDITERRANEAN
SEA

Tyre

Hazor   Karnaim
Meron
Tel Abu Hawam   el-Hammeh
Nazareth

Caesaria
Megiddo   Beth-shan
Samaria Tizrah Succoth
Shechem
Aphek   Shiloh
Gezer   Jericho
Jerusalem   Kirbet Qumran
Bethlehem   Dibon Philadelphia
Lachish   DEAD
SEA
Ascalon
Masada

Eglon

0   20 miles

0   30 kilometers

Archaeological Sites

showed that early people were starting their long, slow march into history. The tale of Israel actually begins with Abraham, Jacob's grandfather, and the other patriarchs. A Muslim tradition says Abraham's oldest son, Ishmael, was the father of the Arab race.

The first Israelites (natives of the ancient kingdom of Israel) probably migrated from Mesopotamia. They were a mixture of races, having fought for their survival against the Assyrians, Egyptians, Canaanites, Amorites, and Babylonians. The Israelites eventually conquered their enemies and strengthened their hold over the land. David and Solomon were two Israelite kings and great politicians described in the Bible.

Jews Hold Masada

The Roman Empire extended its reach to Palestine by 63 B.C. and conquered the region. They ruled the countryside with an iron fist, but the Jews revolted. The rebellion was put down and the Romans destroyed Jerusalem in A.D. 70 as a punishment. A few Jews fled to the desert fortress of Masada, where they held off Roman armies for three years. The last Jewish warriors there killed their own wives and children and committed suicide just at the point of a Roman victory. This hilltop retreat, which now draws many visitors, is reached by a cable car or a long, slow climb up a steep cliffside trail.

The ruins of the ancient fortress of Masada, where Jews held off the Roman armies for three years

Below: **An Armenian priest passes before the Church of the Holy Sepulchre, Jerusalem.**

After the Romans destroyed Jerusalem, the Jews dispersed around the world in what is called the Diaspora. Only a few remained in Palestine, which eventually became part of the Byzantine, or eastern Roman, Empire. In 313, the Roman emperor Constantine declared Christianity the official religion. His mother, Queen Helena, identified many sites associated with the life of Jesus Christ. The Church of the Holy Sepulchre, the Basilica of the Nativity, and other famous shrines that can be visited in Israel today were built then.

From the Ancients to Today **35**

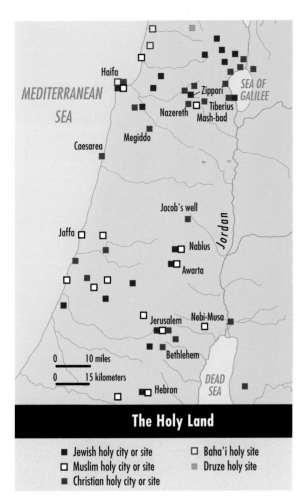

The Holy Land

- Jewish holy city or site
- Muslim holy city or site
- Christian holy city or site
- Baha'i holy site
- Druze holy site

MEDITERRANEAN SEA

Haifa

Zippori
Nazereth
Tiberius
Mash-bad

SEA OF GALILEE

Megiddo

Caesarea

Jacob's well

Jaffa

Nablus

Awarta

Jordan

Jerusalem
Nebi-Musa

Bethlehem

0   10 miles
0   15 kilometers

Hebron

DEAD SEA

Over the next centuries, Muslims, Crusaders from Europe, Egyptian Mamelukes, and other conquerors swept over Palestine. In 1516, the Ottoman Turks captured Jerusalem. They ruled Palestine from 1517 to 1917. The Turks allowed Jews to resettle in Palestine, and by 1845 the largest single community in Jerusalem was again Jewish.

Return to Zion

Organized massacres of Jews in Russia and Poland began in the 1860s. These pogroms encouraged millions of Jews to leave central Europe. Many flocked to western Europe and the Americas. Some Jews thought it would be a good time to "return

Baron Edmond de Rothschild (1854–1934) is considered one of the fathers of the Jewish homeland in Palestine. Almost single-handedly, he funded many of the small agricultural communities there. He was the youngest brother of a famous financial family that traced its roots back to the 1700s in Frankfurt, Germany. Branches of the Rothschild financial empire were established in Austria, England, the United States, and France, as well as in Germany.

to Zion," the Holy Land of their ancestors. They began arriving toward the end of the nineteenth century, eager to start a new life. Many of their communities were supported by the Rothschilds, a banking family.

In 1881, Eliezer Ben-Yehuda moved to Palestine from Lithuania. He dedicated his life to resurrecting the Hebrew language. For centuries, it had been primarily a language of prayer. Ben-Yehuda knew that a common language would unite the Jews. If they kept talking in all their other tongues, he said, it would be difficult for them to communicate. His vision prevailed, and today Hebrew is a national language of Israel.

Opposite: **A guard stands watch at an early Jewish settlement.**

Anti-Jewish Mood Increases

In the 1880s, groups calling themselves *Hoveve-Zion* (Lovers of Zion) formed a movement based on the idea of practical Zionism. A Budapest-born newspaperman named Theodor Herzl who lived in Vienna, Austria, turned this into a political movement. Herzl was worried about the growing tide of anti-Jewish feeling in 1890s Europe. He wrote a pamphlet entitled *Der Judenstaat (The Jewish State)*. In Hebrew, the booklet was called *Tel Aviv (Hill of Spring)*. In 1897, the first Zionist Congress gathered in Basel, Switzerland. Jews from around the world attended, much to Herzl's delight.

Theodor Herzl was an influential advocate of practical Zionism.

More Jews Arrive

More and more Jews came to Palestine. They wanted to be self-sufficient, so they organized communal farms called *kibbutzim* (the singular is *kibbutz*). The first such settlement was founded in 1909 at Degania, near the Sea of Galilee.

Agreements Signed

At the height of World War I (1914–1918), France and Great Britain signed secret agreements with

Degania kibbutz in 1910

The Kibbutz System

The kibbutz system, where all of the property is shared equally by everyone living in a certain village, is unique to Israel. The residents receive no salaries but they are given housing and other necessities, including medical services and education. There are about 230 kibbutzim in Israel. Kibbutzim started at the turn of the century as agricultural cooperatives protected by armed settlers. Most of the modern-day kibbutzim are agricultural, but some make and sell products. Kibbutz hotels are popular vacation spots.

Traditionally, kibbutz children lived together in a separate house away from their parents because their mothers and fathers were working all day. Children visited their parents in the afternoons and on weekends, but they returned to the children's house to sleep. Over the years, this has changed. The youngsters now spend their days with other children but they can sleep with their families at night.

A *moshav* is another type of agricultural settlement, in which families farm their own land and own their own homes. They may market their goods and buy products as a group.

the Arabs. In 1916, they agreed to divide the Ottoman-controlled Middle East into "spheres of influence." Palestine was to be controlled by the British. Britain and France also promised the Arabs they would help them establish their own homelands. A flamboyant, dedicated British soldier, Colonel T. E. Lawrence, better known as Lawrence of Arabia, was sent to the Middle East to organize the Arabs. He molded a strong fighting force against the Ottoman Turks, who were allies of Austria and Germany in the "Great War." His colorfully detailed account of the fighting in Palestine was called *Seven Pillars of Wisdom*. The award-winning film *Lawrence of Arabia* (1962), starring Irish actor Peter O'Toole, was based on his exploits.

British soldier and adventurer T. E. Lawrence in Jerusalem

In 1917, Britain issued the Balfour Declaration, which helped pave the way for a Jewish state. The proclamation, named after the British foreign secretary who wrote it, said that the Jewish people had a right to a "National Home in Palestine." This encouraged thousands of Jews to emigrate to the region after World War I. By the end of the war, Britain had defeated the Turks and captured all of Palestine. Jerusalem fell easily. Two British sergeants were resting outside the Suleiman Gate leading into Old Jerusalem when a local official came out and surrendered.

A plaque there marks the spot, which leads into the Tower of David Citadel, a Roman fortress that is now a museum.

Mandate Given

After World War I, the newly formed League of Nations granted the British authority to govern Palestine—modern-day Israel and Jordan. The first British high commissioner, Sir Herbert Samuel, arrived in 1920. He was a devout Jew and ardent Zionist who was eager to help his fellow Jews. However, he leaned toward the Arabs politically and angered the Zionists when he limited Jewish immigration.

Sir Herbert Samuel *(rear)* **at a 1922 gathering of Armenian priests in Jerusalem**

In 1922, the British divided Palestine, creating the Arab Hashemite Kingdom of TransJordan east of the Jordan River. This is the present-day country of Jordan. The land on the west bank of the river remained "Palestine." Over the next decade, more Jews and Arabs came to Palestine, drawn to the growing prosperity there. The opening of the Hebrew University on Jerusalem's Mount Scopus in 1925 was another positive step taken toward the eventual creation of the state of Israel.

The Zionist movement created the Jewish Agency for Palestine. The organization recruited settlers, helped them find homes and jobs, and organized security when they arrived in their new homeland. This was important because Arabs were fearful of the growing number of Jews. There were riots in Jerusalem, Hebron, and other communities to protest the influx of newcomers. Many Jews and Arabs died.

In 1933, Nazi leader Adolf Hitler came to power in Germany. Under his rule, discrimination and violence against Jews increased in Germany, and more sought relative safety in Palestine. The bloody riots increased. As the street battles spread, the British suggested dividing Palestine into separate but cooperating Arab and Jewish states. In 1939, the British rejected the lofty ideals of the Balfour Declaration and restricted Jewish immigration into Palestine to 25,000 persons to begin with. Then, no more than 10,000 Jews a year were to be admitted over the next five years. After that, none were to be admitted unless the Arabs agreed.

This restriction remained in effect throughout World War II (1939–1945). Even Jews attempting to escape Hitler's Nazis were prevented from entering Palestine. More than 6 million European Jews eventually were murdered in the Holocaust. To help their European brethren, 30,000 Jews in Palestine joined the Jewish Brigade, a unit of the British Army. They received valuable military training that benefited them later as they began fighting for their independence.

Jewish children in search of a home arriving in Palestine in 1947

Refugee Ships Halted

After the war, U.S. president Harry S. Truman asked Britain to allow 100,000 Holocaust survivors to enter Palestine. The British refused and halted refugee ships. Thousands of Jews were interned on the Mediterranean island of Cyprus while the British tried to figure out what to do with them. Many were eventually smuggled out to Palestine on leaky old ships. Zionist terrorist groups attacked British troops in Palestine and blew up the King David Hotel, where the high commissioner had his offices. Ninety-one people were killed in the blast.

Chaim Weizmann is sworn in as the first president of Israel.

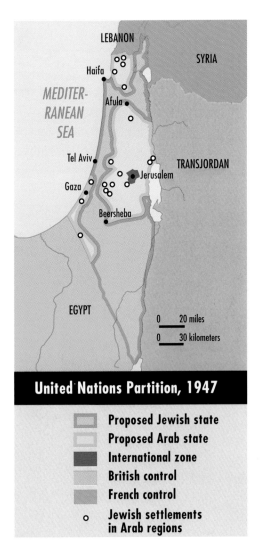

United Nations Partition, 1947

- Proposed Jewish state
- Proposed Arab state
- International zone
- British control
- French control
- ○ Jewish settlements in Arab regions

In 1947, Britain renounced its mandate to govern Palestine and asked the United Nations (UN) to seek a solution to the region's political woes. On November 29, the UN General Assembly agreed to create a Jewish state in Palestine. The Arabs rejected the plan and civil war broke out. Despite the fighting, the independent State of Israel was announced on May 14, 1948. Israel was immediately invaded by Iraq, Syria, Egypt, Jordan, and Lebanon, but the Israelis beat back their enemies. In 1949, Israel signed armistice agreements with Syria, Egypt, Jordan, and Lebanon. A period of relative calm followed in which Israel's economy mushroomed.

The next war was fought in the Sinai Desert in 1956, after Egypt took over the Suez Canal, which was owned primarily by Great Britain and

France. In response, Israel attacked Egypt. Britain and France also attacked Egypt, a few days later. The UN ended the fighting and sent in peacekeeping troops. In 1967, when the UN peacekeepers left, Egypt sent soldiers into the Sinai and blocked access to the Israeli port of Eilat. Israel then attacked Egypt on June 5, 1967. Syria, Jordan, and Iraq joined Egypt but they were all defeated. This famous "Six-Day War" resulted in a reunited Jerusalem. The Israelis took over the Gaza Strip, the Sinai, and the Golan Heights and occupied the West Bank. This enraged the Arab League, a group of Arab countries, which vowed no peace with Israel.

Egyptian soldiers wounded and captured in the Six-Day War

Israel was in a state of siege. There were plane hijackings and a massacre of Israeli athletes at the 1972 Olympic Games in Munich, West Germany. On the Jewish holiday of Yom Kippur in 1973, Egypt and Syria attacked Israel along the Suez and the Golan Heights. Israel was able to push back the Egyptians and Syrians. In an effort to resolve the situation, Egyptian leader Anwar el-Sadat went to Jerusalem in 1977 to talk with Israeli prime minister Menachem Begin.

In 1978, U.S. president Jimmy Carter got the Israelis and the Arabs to compromise on some issues. Prime Minister Begin and President Sadat signed an "accord" at Camp David. A peace treaty between Israel and Egypt was signed in Paris in 1979. Due to their efforts to bring peace to the region,

An Arab hijacker is escorted from a jetliner by an Israeli soldier disguised as an airline technician.

Begin and Sadat received the Nobel Peace Prize in 1978.

In 1982, Israel pulled out of the Sinai. The same year, however, Israel invaded Lebanon to protect its northern settlements from Palestinian terrorist attacks. The UN stepped in to replace Israeli troops in Lebanon. By 1985, the only Israeli presence there was along a security strip between the two countries.

Egyptian president Anwar el-Sadat, U.S. president Jimmy Carter, and Israeli prime minister Menachem Begin signing the Camp David Accords in 1978

In 1987, the *intifada* (an Arabic word meaning "uprising") began. This was a violent protest by Palestinians against Israel's military occupation of the Gaza Strip and the Jordan's West Bank. Rocks thrown at Israeli soldiers soon escalated to bombs and bullets. Dozens of people were killed. The intifada influenced Israeli elections, affected the economy, and made Israelis worry about their security. As a result, it forced the government to take another look at its relations with the Palestinians. By 1991, everyone was ready to talk seriously. Peace talks were held in Madrid, Spain, that October. These talks marked the first time the Palestinian Arabs and the Israelis sat down face to face. They agreed that a Palestinian Authority would be responsible for the Gaza Strip and Jericho. Israeli leaders went to Morocco to thank King Hassan for assisting in the negotiations.

On September 13, 1993, the world's photographers recorded the handshake of Israeli prime minister Yitzhak Rabin and Yasser Arafat, head of the Palestine Liberation Organization (PLO). After long days of successful peace talks at Camp David in the United States, the two were hosted at the White House by President Bill Clinton. The greeting between the two set off a positive chain of events in the Middle East. Jordan and Israel signed a peace treaty on October 26, 1994. The Syrians, who had long supported the Palestinian cause, also launched talks with Israel to resolve their differences.

Israeli prime minister Yitzhak Rabin and Palestine Liberation Organization leader Yasser Arafat shake hands following successful peace talks hosted by U.S. president Bill Clinton.

However, terrorist attacks by Palestinian Muslim extremists continued in Jerusalem and Tel Aviv into 1996. The Palestinians were frustrated by the slow pace of implementing the agreements made by both sides during the previous peace talks.

In October 1998, representatives of Israel, the Palestinians, and Jordan met beside the Wye River in Maryland to discuss security and land issues in the region. U.S. president Bill Clinton was also on hand to help in the negotiations. Under the resulting Wye River Memorandum, the Palestinian Authority is to dismantle the infrastructure (operational system) of terrorist groups. The Palestinians are also to confiscate illegal weapons and jail up to thirty convicted terrorists who were free in Palestinian territory. In return, the Israelis are to pull back from more territory they hold on the West Bank. The accord will succeed only if certain steps are taken according to a set timeline of "you do this, and I do that." Where this will lead Israel and its neighbors can only be answered as time wears on.

A market in Jerusalem following a suicide bombing by two Palestinian militants

CHAPTER

FIVE

Birth and Growth of a Nation

Look back to the late 1940s. World War II had just ended and Holocaust survivors were struggling to reach Palestine. In November 1947, the United Nations passed a resolution to divide British-controlled Palestine into separate Jewish and Arab states. The Jewish portion would be a republic, a state in which the power rests with citizens entitled to vote and who are represented by elected officials.

THE U.S. AND BRITISH GOVERNments wanted David Ben-Gurion, chairman of the executive group of the Zionist Organization, to delay an announcement of the new country for another six months. They were worried about continuing warfare in the region and did not want to stir up Arab nationalism. Nor did they want to become directly involved in a conflict there.

Ben-Gurion knew that timing was important. His military advisers told him that his new state would have only a fifty-fifty chance of surviving impending attacks by its Arab neighbors. The Jews had waited for this moment for 1,878 years, ever since the Romans expelled their ancestors from ancient Israel. Therefore, in the spring of 1948, an eager Ben-Gurion chose a site for announcing Israel's Declaration of Independence. The location of the 32-minute ceremony was to be kept secret until the last minute for fear of sabotage.

David Ben-Gurion declares the State of Israel in 1948.

Opposite: The Israeli flag flies over the ancient seaport of Caesarea.

Ben-Gurion selected a bunkerlike building built in 1911 that had been the home of Meir Dizengoff, Tel Aviv's first mayor. In 1936, the house was enlarged to become the city's art museum. The building was not quite prepared for the birth of a nation. Chairs were borrowed from a coffeehouse, carpets from a carpet store, and a microphone from a nearby shop. A portrait of Theodor Herzl, founder of the Zionist movement, hung on a wall. On both sides of the picture were new Israeli flags.

Israel's national flag is white with a blue hexagram (six-pointed star) called the *Magen David* (Shield of David). The star is centered between two equal horizontal blue bands near the top and bottom edges of the flag. A similar flag was displayed at the Boston Benei Zion Society meeting in 1891, using the two blue stripes, the white center, and the Shield of David. In 1933, the Shield of David was added for the 18th Zionist Congress. British prime minister Winston Churchill ordered that the flag become the official banner for the Jewish Brigade in World War II. Six months after independence, the flag of the Zionist movement was made the state flag.

The official emblem and coat of arms of the state is the *menorah*, or candelabrum, the ancient symbol of the Jewish people. The menorah is surrounded by olive branches, linked at the bottom by Hebrew letters that spell "Israel."

The room was ready, yet there remained one challenge. What would the new country be named? This dispute was resolved barely thirty minutes before the independence ceremony was to begin on May 14, 1948. Some politicians in the Provisional Council of State wanted to call the country "Zion." Others wanted "Judea." Still others thought "State of the Jews" was best. But the majority chose *"Medinat Yisrael"* (State of Israel).

Thousands of people crowded Rothschild Boulevard in downtown Tel Aviv to witness history in the making. After the dignitaries were seated, Ben-Gurion described Israel's goals and dreams as an independent country and its desire for peace with the Arabs. He concluded by saying, *"Zot Medinat Yisrael"* ("This is the state of Israel"). Next came Tel Aviv's chief rabbi, reciting the *Shehecheyanu*, a prayer thanking God for "bringing us to this time." On that uplifting note, Israel greeted the world.

"Hatikvah" ("The Hope")

Hatikvah ("The Hope"), the national anthem of Israel, was written as a poem by Naphtali Herz Imber in 1878. Samuel Cohen set the poem to music a few years later, basing the tune on an old Moldavian-Romanian folk song.

*As long as deep in the heart
The soul of a Jew yearns.
And towards the East
An eye looks to Zion*

*Our hope is not yet lost
The hope of two thousand years
To be a free people in our land
The land of Zion and Jerusalem.*

Governmental Influences

The country's government has been influenced by several important factors, including Western European parliamentary democracies, Eastern and Central European political institutions, Middle Eastern customs, and Jewish tradition. Israel is proud of its elected government, numerous political parties, independent judges, free press, and civilian rule.

Yet Israel is one of the six nations in the 185-member United Nations that do not have a written constitution. In 1949, the first Knesset (parliament) enacted a Transition Law, sometimes called Israel's "small constitution." The politicians feared that a full-blown, written constitution would start a conflict between religious and state authorities. Even Ben-Gurion was opposed to a written constitution, saying that the Declaration of Independence should be the first step in the evolution of a state and that a body of laws and rights would gradually follow.

In 1950, it was agreed that such a document would be built chapter by chapter upon the enactment of Basic Laws. These laws were the basis for the organization of Israeli government and its citizens' rights. The Basic Laws can be changed only by a special majority of at least 80 members of the 120-member Knesset.

State's Supreme Authority

The Knesset is a unicameral (one-house) parliament and the supreme authority of the state. Its members are elected from a party list by voters for a four-year term. The party with the

The Knesset

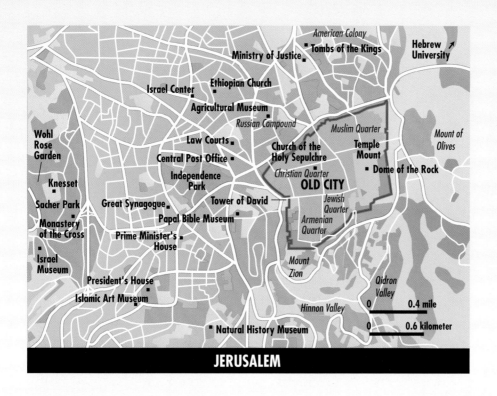

JERUSALEM

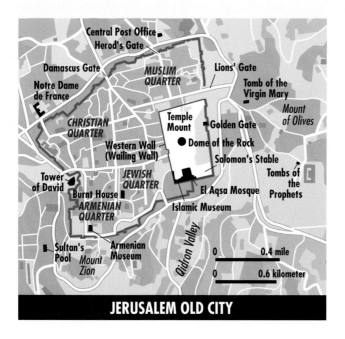

JERUSALEM OLD CITY

Jerusalem: Did You Know This?

Jerusalem has been settled almost continuously for more than 3,000 years under different names. It was made the capital of modern Israel in 1950. Located on two rocky hills, the city contains important Jewish, Christian, and Muslim holy sites.

Population: 602,100 residents (1996; includes East Jerusalem)

Altitude: 2,500 feet (762 m) above sea level

Location: 35 miles (56 km) east of the Mediterranean coast and 15 miles (24 km) west of the Dead Sea

Average daily temperature: January, 50°F (10°C); July, 74°F (23°C)

most votes also gets extra seats according to a complicated formula. The Knesset passes legislation, helps form national policy, is responsible for budgets, keeps an eye on cabinet members, and debates issues. It works through eleven permanent committees ranging from foreign affairs to education. A speaker is appointed to preside over the Knesset, which holds at least two sessions a year.

Head of State

The president is the head of state in Israel. Any Israeli citizen is eligible to run for the office. The president is elected to a five-year term through secret balloting by a majority of the Knesset. Israeli presidents cannot serve more than two terms. This is an important ceremonial position. The president signs treaties and laws enacted by the Knesset and appoints diplomats, judges, and the governor of the Bank of Israel.

Prime Minister Golda Meir *(right)* with Defense Minister Moshe Dayan

The prime minister is head of the government, as well as head of the cabinet. This is similar to the British government. Women have long played a responsible role in the country's affairs. Prime Minister Golda Meir (1898–1978) is an example. She was born in Kiev, Russia; raised in Milwaukee, Wisconsin; and emigrated to Palestine in the 1920s. Meir was long active in politics, becoming prime minister in 1969 and resigning in 1974, when she retired from politics.

Campaign posters line a sidewalk.

The cabinet is the top executive policy-making body in Israel. It is usually made up of members of the majority party or a coalition of several parties. Just as in Great Britain, the cabinet introduces legislation, which is then voted upon by the Knesset members after going through various committees for revision.

The two largest parties are the center-liberal Labor Party and the more conservative Likud (Unity) Party. There are numerous smaller parties. In the past, most Arab Israelis affiliated with the Labor Party. The amount of support given by these various parties determines the strength or weakness of a prime minister. A government can be replaced if the parties object to a prime minister's policies.

Rabin's Murder

The tragic murder of Prime Minister Yitzhak Rabin in 1995 presented serious challenges to the Israeli government. Some conservative Israelis had objected to Rabin pursuing peace with Israel's Arab neighbors. They did not want to compromise on giving up land that they felt was historically theirs to people they considered enemies. Rabin wanted to continue negotiations, and he was assassinated on November 4, 1995, by an Israeli who objected to the peace process. A memorial in Tel Aviv marks the spot where he was killed.

Rabin's successor, Prime Minister Benjamin Netanyahu of the Likud Party, took a hard line. He allowed the building of Israeli settlements on disputed land. Some of his supporters did not want to talk to the Arabs at all. Other Israelis actively sought peace. What one person considered progress, another

(Left to right) PLO chairman Yasser Arafat, Israeli foreign minister Shimon Peres, and Israeli prime minister Yitzhak Rabin display their shared Nobel Peace Prize awards.

saw as treason. This frustrated the Palestinians and the Arabs, who felt that they had a friend in Rabin. Compounding the problem from the Arab side were some militants who called for a *jihad* (holy war) in which believers in Islam would eventually "liberate" Palestine from the Jews.

Steps Taken Together

Fortunately, Israel and its former enemies are taking some positive steps to resolve their differences. The Israeli Army now conducts joint patrols with the Palestinian forces in a security zone between Israel and Palestinian-occupied territory. Small steps have been taken toward normalization of relations with Syria. A peace treaty has

Prime Minister Benjamin Netanyahu

been signed with Jordan. In 1998, King Hussein of Jordan presented a million-dollar gift to the families of several Israeli schoolchildren killed by a Jordanian border guard in March the preceding year. The king also offered his sympathy and apologies over the tragedy.

The Court System

Israelis turn to their court system for help. The Supreme Court, the highest judicial forum in the country, is seen as guarding the values of freedom and justice as they are viewed in the Western world.

Justice

In the Bible, the image of justice is described as a circle and associated with the sky. "Justice reflects from the sky," says Psalms 85:12. Justice is like a circle, a value that can be pursued, but never reached, according to tradition. But law is a man-made "line," and therefore subject to the changing perceptions of the world. By means of circles and straight lines, the graceful Israeli Supreme Court building reflects those biblical ideas in its gates, walls, windows, judges' chambers, and courtrooms. The facility was designed by brother and sister architects Ada Karmi Melamede and Ram Karmi of Tel Aviv.

Supreme Court rulings are binding—the last word in any dispute. The Supreme Court can even review the decisions of the powerful religious courts. As the High Court of Justice, it also hears petitions by people who live in Judea, Samaria, and other areas occupied by the Israeli Army.

The court usually consists of three judges, but up to eleven can serve. The judges sit in the Supreme Court Building, one of the major office centers in the heart of West Jerusalem.

The court system includes military and civil courts as well as special courts for traffic, insurance, juvenile, labor, and municipal operations. The courts are responsible to their respective ministries. Demonstrating the many influences on the Israeli legal system, laws applicable to Israeli Jews fall under the *halakah,* Jewish religious law. U.S. legal tradition has influenced civil-rights cases. British law provides the base for criminal law and the court procedure. Arab tribal laws, the *Koran* (the Muslim holy book), and the French Napoleonic Code also affect the legal system. A lawyer in Israel must be highly skilled to maneuver through this mixture of heritages.

Local Government

For local government, Israel has six administrative districts called *mehozot.* (The singular form is *mahoz.*) The Central, Haifa, Jerusalem, Northern, Southern, and Tel Aviv mehozot are managed by district commissioners. Fourteen subdistricts are coordinated by district officers. These officials are appointed by the minister of the interior. They draft local legislation, set tax rates and budgets, and approve public works projects. Mayors and members of municipal councils are elected.

Israel has several "national institutions." These are semi-official organizations such as the Jewish Agency, the World Zionist Organization, and the *Histadrut* (the General Federation of Labor). They help with fund-raising for Zionist causes, education, cultural projects, and social welfare. About 90 percent of all Israeli workers belong to the Histadrut. Similar to these organizations, but acting independently, are private groups overseas. The New Israel Fund, the Peace Now Organization, and dozens of others help with environmental issues, advocate religious tolerance, promote civil rights, or encourage continuing peace talks.

The Business of Business Is Business

Israel's business world is as colorful and diverse as its culture. Its economy includes a wide range of products and services. Tourism is a major source of income, amounting to approximately $2.6 billion in 1996.

New homes are built next to farm fields.

Opposite: **Harvesting melons in the south**

An Arab woman tends almond trees on the West Bank.

THE FIRST SETTLERS IN Palestine worked hard turning the barren landscape into an oasis of flowering beauty. But with the growth of cities and expanding industries, agriculture has stepped into the background.

Farming Is Important

Farming remains important although barely 4 percent of the labor force still works in agriculture. During peak planting and harvesting time, seasonal workers from Eastern Europe and Thailand and other Asian countries are brought in to help. In addition, more than 20,000 Palestinians from the Gaza Strip and other Palestinian-controlled lands work on Israeli farms.

Poultry, dairy, beef, vegetables, cotton, citrus, and other fruits make up Israel's agricultural palette. With the exception of some grains, Israel is self-sufficient in its food production. It exports citrus fruits and other commodities around the world. Many of the oranges, melons, kiwis, and mangoes

**Picking eggplants on
a kibbutz**

What Israel Grows, Makes, and Mines

Agriculture (1997)

Watermelons	450,000 metric tons
Tomatoes	440,000 metric tons
Grapefruit	390,000 metric tons

Mining (1996)

Potash	2,500,000 metric tons
Phosphate rock	2,450,000 metric tons

Manufacturing

Cement (1996)	6,723,000 metric tons
Cardboard and paper (1996)	227,681 metric tons
Polyethylene (1993)	144,147 metric tons
Wine (1993)	12,733,000 liters

---

seen in European, Canadian, and U.S. grocery stores come from Israel. Long-stemmed roses, carnations, and other flowers are also grown year-round in greenhouses and sold in Europe, amounting to a quarter of Israel's agricultural exports. Some of the finest vineyards in the world can also be found in Israel. Israeli wines are admired for their special zing.

Tractors Chug

The Golan Heights were a battlefield in 1967. Today, tractors chug across the rich landscape where tanks once roared. The Golan shows astounding agricultural development. Apricots,

An Israeli soldier under fire in the Golan Heights in 1973

nectarines, grapefruits, plums, bananas, avocados, dates, and mangoes are grown in the south. To the north, farmers cultivate cherries, apples, blueberries, and pears. Most of the fruit consumed in Israel is provided by these farms. The main field crops here include corn, onions, tomatoes, and cotton. Israeli farmers also raise potatoes for the tons of french fries served at the fifty-three McDonald's restaurants in Israel as well as the many local chain restaurants.

There are questions about the political future of this region. The Golan Heights and the West Bank have Israel's richest farmland. The territory was captured by the Israeli Army during the Six-Day War in 1967. But some of it may be returned to Syria and the Palestinian Authority as peace negotiations continue between Israel and its Arab neighbors.

Until the changeover, farm life goes on as usual. Cows and sheep graze on the pastures, while turkeys and chickens are raised in pens. Poultry consumption in Israel is among the highest in the world.

Settlers in the Golan Heights use horses to manage their herds.

From Chile to Israel

Some unusual farm animals live in Israel today. Ilan Diver has the only alpaca ranch in the Middle East. He raises alpacas he brought from Chile to a ranch near Mitzpe Ramon in the Negev Desert. These llama-like creatures are raised for their fine wool. Diver sells the wool to buyers in Japan, as well as to tourists who drop by his ranch to admire his herd of 300 animals. His original herd of 175 was flown to Israel in 1990.

There are no big lakes or rivers in Israel, and no underground water reservoirs. As a result, important questions are raised over the limited water supply. Farming and agriculture use almost four-fifths of the water supply. Therefore, should the country import more food so that less water is used directly for agriculture? This would save more water for industry. But how much industry can Israel support?

Few Sources of Water

The major water sources in Israel are the narrow Jordan River, the Sea of Galilee, and a few smaller rivers. Each year, the average rainfall is 28 inches (71 cm) in the north and 8 inches (20 cm) in the south. This presents a problem for agriculture, making it necessary to use the precious water for crop irrigation. An intricate system of pipes, tunnels, dams, pumping stations, canals, and reservoirs brings water from the north and central regions to the arid south.

Foreign Aid

In 1998, Israel said it planned on phasing out the $1.2 billion in annual aid it receives from the United States. Prime Minister Benjamin Netanyahu said he wanted his country to become more self-sufficient. The phasing out will take about a decade. In the late 1990s, Israel was receiving nearly 40 percent of all U.S. aid. In return for scaling back on the economic front, Israel asked for another $600 million in defense assistance.

This canal provides water for crop irrigation.

For irrigated agriculture to be possible, Israel has to be very efficient and conserve what little water there is. Israel imports crops that need lots of water from other countries and cultivates crops that need less water.

Israel also has new strategies for the treatment of water in the Jordan Valley. The country treats and reuses wastewater and desalinates saline (salty) spring water. Desalination is a process that removes the salt from saltwater to make it drinkable.

These limited resources are a constant source of conflict in the Middle East. For centuries, nations have argued and fought over control of the Jordan River. However, they are slowly learning to work together. Since signing a peace treaty in the early 1990s, Israel and Jordan have viewed water as a shared resource. Since both face shortages, they realized they needed to collaborate on water-storage projects and to establish antipollution policies to improve water quality.

Tourism

Tourism is one of Israel's top industries. Every year, about 2 million visitors travel to Israel. Some come for the culture and sunny climate. History attracts others. Still others are religious pilgrims. Muslims, Christians, and Jews visit sites that are sacred in their religions. The Dead Sea region has been a popular resort area since ancient times. Its year-round sunshine, its clean air, and the healing properties of its

Tourists enjoy mud baths at Dead Sea resorts.

mineral-rich waters continue to draw visitors from around the world. The mineral-rich mud can alleviate skin ailments. Some spas offer special beauty packages with massages and mud packs.

The United States has been Israel's biggest trading partner since 1985. There is also a strong business bond between Israel and Western Europe because they are geographically close. And Japan and China exchange steel products, heavy equipment, fish, and other products for Israeli high-tech equipment, chemicals, and other industrial goods.

Exports

Israel also exports cut diamonds, airplanes, high-technology products, ships, wood and paper products, and textiles. Diamond cutting and polishing, high-tech electronics, textiles, apparel, and chemical products are among the leading industries. The manufacturing of military and transport equipment, metal products, and electrical equipment add up to economic success. The more recently developed Golan Heights area adds an edge to the economy because of new industries sprouting up in plastics, electro-optics, defense systems, dairy products, chemicals, telecommunications, computer hardware, food packaging, shoes, and research and development. Mining is big along the Dead Sea shores, yielding a treasure of potash, magnesium chloride, and bromine. There is so much mining here that it is affecting the depth of the water.

A tank assembly line

Potash is produced from carnallite mined along the Dead Sea.

Currency Facts

Israel's official currency is the new Israeli shekel, or *sheqel* (NIS). (The plural is *sheqalim*.) In 1999, one U.S. dollar was equal to 4.09 NIS and one Canadian dollar was equal to 2.74 NIS. One hundred new *agorot*, which are like pennies, equal one shekel.

Banknotes come in denominations of 10, 20, 50, 100, and 200. There are 1-shekel, 5- and 10-sheqalim, and 5-, 10-, 50-, and 100-agorot coins. The front of the 20-sheqalim note features a picture of Moshe Sharet (Israel's second prime minister), the Israeli flag, and Herzeliyah High School. The 50-sheqalim note has a picture of the writer Shmuel Yosef Agnon backed by books and buildings. The 100-sheqalim note shows a portrait of Yitzhak Ben-Zvi, Israel's second president, backed by a village and a group of people.

Thousands Employed

The country's economy is soaring. The Tel Aviv Stock Exchange is always busy, with traders dealing in lucrative big-money stocks on the Mishtanim stock index and the Karam index of smaller companies. Israel is a hardworking country, with about 2 million skilled employees. Almost 75 percent of the workers have service jobs. The country's 19,000 industries employ 22 percent of the workers. Israel's unemployment rate is 6.4 percent, one of the lowest in the world. The country's industrial output was second-highest in the world, after Korea, between 1990 and 1994. Fourteen percent of the workforce are graduates of universities or technical colleges.

Their bustle is seen everywhere, from the Weizmann Institute of Science in Rehovot, south of Tel Aviv, where semi-conductor crystals are made, to the Phil tobacco factory in Rosh-Ha-Aayin. In the past ten years, Israel's high-tech industries have grown quickly. Computer industries are doing so well and have attracted so much international interest that Israel is nicknamed "the Second Silicon Valley," referring to the area in California where many computer products are made.

Overseas companies are encouraged to invest in Israel. Subsequently, many foreign firms do business there.

Traders on the Tel Aviv Stock Exchange

It seems that almost everyone in Israel has a cell phone, from the desert Bedouin to the corporate executive. The Israel Communications Corporation is responsible for regulating the phone system. The Postal Authority makes communications policy, handles licensing, and supervises communications services.

The Israel Broadcasting Authority directs one national television network, five national radio networks, and one short-wave radio network for overseas. In addition, the Israel Defense Forces operate their own radio system. In 1993, cable TV was introduced to Israel. Soon, 60 percent of the country was hooked up.

Cell phones are used all over Israel.

Israel has launched two satellites for military use and a third for private purposes.

Israelis love to read. They delve into magazines covering entertainment, sports, fashion, the arts, and other subjects.

Everyone rushes to get their daily newspapers, published in Hebrew, Russian, Arabic, Yiddish, English, Hungarian, French, German, or Polish. Some newspapers are affiliated with political parties. The major independent English-language daily paper is the *Jerusalem Post*. The principal Arabic-language daily is *Al Anba (The News)*. *Ma'ariv (Evening)* and *Yediot Aharonot (Latest News)* are the primary Hebrew-language daily newspapers. There are also many weekly papers.

Transportation Systems

It is easy to get around Israel, with its 9,134 miles (14,700 km) of paved highways. Major rail lines, used mostly for freight, cover 322 miles (520 km), linking major cities and industrial areas. A rapid-transit urban rail system is being planned for Tel Aviv after the year 2000. Buses are the most popular public transport.

There are fifty-seven civilian and military airports in the country. The national commercial airline is El Al. Conforming to Jewish law, the food on board El Al flights is kosher and the line does not fly on the Sabbath. When it is time to pray on El Al flights, Orthodox men gather in groups of ten or more for services at the front or rear of their plane, as they would in a synagogue. Numerous other international airlines also serve Israel.

Haifa is Israel's main port. Other ports include Ashdod, Ashqelon, Eilat, Hadera, and Tel Aviv-Jaffa. Ferry services run to and from Greece, Cyprus, and Italy. Israel is easy to reach—for pleasure or for business.

Getting Around

Sherut taxis are shared cabs, often the size of minivans, that operate on fixed routes within cities and to and from Ben-Gurion Airport. Regular cabs can be picked up outside hotels, bus and train stations, and at the airport. Urban buses operate regularly in the cities, but there is no service on the Sabbath. To save money, many young people hitchhike in Israel. It is not uncommon to see groups of schoolchildren or soldiers loaded down with military gear thumbing a ride.

A People Potpourri

Israel has almost 6 million citizens, 85 percent of whom are Jews. Muslims, Druze, and Christians make up most of the rest of the population. When Israel was founded in 1948, thousands of Jews from around the world emigrated to their new nation. They brought their skills, traditions, and cultures from the Far East, Africa, Europe, and the Americas. Israel is a melting pot of heritages.

BEFORE 1948, MOST OF THE JEWISH SETTLERS IN what was Palestine came from Central and Eastern Europe. Often they came to escape religious persecution and sought safety in the Holy Land. Palestine was rough and mostly barren at the turn of the nineteenth century but the settlers worked diligently to make the desert flower. After World War II, almost 2 million Jews came from North Africa, Ethiopia, and Arab lands such as Yemen, adding even more spice to the ethnic stew. In the 1990s, hundreds of thousands of Russians made up another great wave of newcomers. In addition, highly educated Jews from Canada, the United States, South Africa, and other countries have come to live in their spiritual homeland.

This woman's heritage is European.

Trouble Flared

Most newcomers were well received. However, trouble sometimes flared up between established Israelis and the new arrivals because of their different culture or their inability to speak Hebrew. Competition for jobs has also been a disruptive factor. Numerous Jews from India came to Israel in the 1950s and 1960s. Many were highly capable managers, accountants, and engineers who spoke

Many Jews came to Israel from Ethiopia.

Opposite: **A Jewish family in Jaffa**

A People Potpourri **77**

The Knesset passed a resolution guaranteeing the rights of Jews from India.

English. Yet at first, even some of the most skilled Indian workers were restricted to low-paying, dead-end jobs. Charges of racism and discrimination resulted in civil-rights marches and demonstrations. Some ultra-Orthodox Israelis did not consider the Indians to be Jews because they were not familiar with all the strict Judaic traditions. To resolve the problem, the Knesset passed a resolution saying the Indian immigrants were Jews in all respects and had the same rights as other Jews. Eventually, many Indian Jews found their talents needed in the fast-growing Israeli aircraft and electronics industries.

Why Choose Israel?

A typical new Israeli arrival is Jonathan Rosenblum, a graduate of Yale Law School. He grew up in a Jewish family in Illinois. He and his wife came to Israel on their honeymoon and decided to stay. "I asked myself, what was the power that would allow these people to preserve their sense of identity as Jews, after being scattered around the world. My idea was that it was a connectedness to God. So I felt I had to be here," he says.

A trained lawyer, Rosenblum now writes biographies of Jewish scholars and produces a regular column on Orthodox religious affairs for the *Jerusalem Post* newspaper. His wife is a psychiatric social worker. The couple has eight children. Four of Rosenblum's five brothers also now live in Israel.

Native-born Israelis call themselves *sabras*, after a cactus that thrives in the desert.

Native-born "Sabras"

As Israel edged toward the year 2000, finally more than 50 percent of its citizens were native-born. The Israeli natives are proud to call themselves *sabras*, literally meaning "prickly pears." Prickly pears are plants that are prickly on the outside but sweet on the inside. These tough little plants can grow anywhere in the Middle East's harsh climate and poor soil. Just like the prickly pear, the Israelis have flourished. This is a country of young people, with 29 percent of the population 14 years old or younger. Another 61 percent are between 15 and 64. Only 10 percent are older than 65.

Israel's Population

Total population: 5,987,000 (1998 estimate); this includes 136,000 Israeli settlers in the West Bank, 15,000 in the Golan Heights, 5,000 in the Gaza Strip, and 156,000 in East Jerusalem.

Ethnic breakdown:

Jewish, 81%

Non-Jewish (mostly Arab), 19%

Population distribution in Israel

Persons per sq. mi.		Persons per sq. km.
more than 2500		more than 1000
1300–2500		500–1000
500–1300		200–500
25–500		10–200
fewer than 25		fewer than 10

Studying at yeshiva, a religious school for Jews

There are state, state religious, and independent schools in Israel. About 70 percent of Israeli children attend the nonreligious schools. There is a separate Arab and Druze school system. Youngsters from age five to sixteen must attend school. Everyone needs at least ten years of education in addition to preschool. There are several levels of classes in the secular education system, similar to those in Canada and the United States. Primary education runs from grades one through six. Grades seven through nine are junior high school. Students in tenth through twelfth grade attend high school. There are three types of high schools—general academic schools, where classes are taught in history, math, languages, social studies, geography, and economics; vocational schools; and agricultural schools. Vocational and agricultural high schools offer courses that lead to engineering or technical diplomas.

Primary school students

High school students between classes

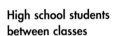

Admission standards are high for Israel's universities.

Courses Approved

The Ministry of Culture and Education is responsible for licensing teachers and approving the courses. It shares these roles with the ministries of labor and agriculture for the technical schools. It is necessary to pass a tough national exam in order to go to university. There are seven universities in Israel: the Israel Institute of Technology, Hebrew University in Jerusalem, Tel Aviv University, Bar-Ilan University, Haifa University, Ben-Gurion University of the Negev, and the post-graduate Weizmann Institute of Science. The campuses are packed with young and old Israelis and exchange students from other countries. Streets near the campuses are crowded with motorbikes and bicycles. Buses constantly load and unload book-laden students. Nearby neighborhoods overflow with trendy coffee shops and well-stocked bookstores.

In the 1950s and 1960s, a Jewish Consciousness Program was installed in the nonreligious schools. The program was intended to teach youngsters what it means to be Jewish. But the hard lessons learned during Israel's wars probably did more to emphasize Jewish consciousness than any textbook could ever do.

Field Trips

Schoolchildren take field trips to Jewish holy sites and to military museums where veterans tell their stories. Bringing one fateful chapter to life in their national story is Yad Vashem, the Museum of the Holocaust in Jerusalem. The complex provides a somber look at the horrors inflicted on the Jews by the Nazis and their allies in Europe in the 1930s and 1940s. The museum sits on a hilltop overlooking a quiet valley filled with

The unfinished columns of the Children's Memorial at Yad Vashem represent unfinished lives.

memorials to destroyed villages. Around the museum are trees planted in memory of "The Righteous," non-Jews who helped Jews escape the Nazis. Nobody talks very loudly after going through Yad Vashem.

Children's Memorial

An underground chamber at the museum is dedicated to children who died in the Holocaust. The chamber is lit by a few candles, whose flames are reflected by mirrors a hundred times over as tiny pinpoints of stars. In the background, you can hear the soft cries and moans of children and a repeated whispered reading of hundreds of names of the dead.

Muslim Arabs are Israel's second-largest ethnic group. Most belong to the Sunni sect and live in villages throughout Galilee. They have their own schools in the Israeli school system. The Arabs also have their own political parties, businesses, and local administrators. The Muslims follow their own calendar and observe their own festivals and holy days.

Residents Mix

Jaffa, an ancient Mediterranean seaport next to Tel Aviv, has a large number of Arab residents who have mixed well with the Jewish population. It was not always this way. During the war following independence, Jaffa was captured by Israeli troops after bloody street fighting. That is all in the past now. After parties at Jaffa's Sinai Club and other hot spots, Jewish, Muslim, and Christian young people like to congregate around a sweet-smelling bakery in the old city. There they can always

It's night
All is calm
The birds
Still send
Some cries
to their comrades and
To the sun
Night has come
Like a curtain that is drawn
Slowly, slowly.
Night is born
Words on a black cloud
Here is the moon
And in the rooms
They sleep with glimpses
Of dreams in their eyes.
—poem by Fanny Ben-Aris, age 9, concentration camp inmate; displayed at Yad Vashem

A young Arab boy from the West Bank

After the Romans destroyed
Jerusalem in the year 70,
surviving Jews fled. The
Nahum Goldmann Museum
of the Jewish Diaspora at
Tel Aviv University traces
this dispersal of Jews
around the world. Jewish
communities took root
everywhere, even in such
remote locales as Fiji
and Haiti.

No matter where they
found themselves, the Jews
dreamed of their own
land. "The land of Israel,
the blessing of its soil
embraced the home of the
Jew—wherever he dwelt,"
says a prayer that is read
during the Feast of Sukkot.

get a snack before heading home. The shop is run by an Israeli Arab family long active in politics and community affairs. The crowded street outside the tiny shop shows the bright face of a new Israel, a face of many complexions, beliefs, and heritages.

Language Influences

Hebrew and Arabic are the official languages of Israel. Hebrew was spoken by the ancient Israelites in the biblical era. Some of its sounds are formed toward the back of the throat, giving Hebrew a guttural sound. The language is similar to others spoken in the Middle East. It is believed that today's Hebrew has its roots with the Canaanites who inhabited Canaan (Palestine) centuries before the Israelites arrived. In fact, the Israelites called their language "the speech of Canaan." Later, when the Kingdom of Judah was founded, the language was known as Judean. However, scholars now know that there were some slight differences between the Hebrew dialects spoken in the area. Most of the Old Testament of the Bible was written in Hebrew.

Over the centuries, the Jewish people were influenced by other cultures of the region, whose language was Aramaic. Hebrew became more of a "classical" language, used in religious services and by scholars, poets, and authors. Aramaic became the language of the ordinary people. These influences left room for much interpretation of words, depending on how they were pronounced and written. Translating manuscripts written long ago is very difficult because of the way words and meanings have changed over the centuries.

In one edition of *Ariel*, a leading Israeli literary magazine, publisher Asher Weil asked his writers to discuss the changing nature of Hebrew as a living language. In an article, Druze poet Salman Mashalah said:

I write in the Hebrew language
which is not my mother tongue, to
lose myself in the world. He who doesn't
get lost, will never find the whole.

Yiddish Spoken Here

Some older Israelis still speak Yiddish, used by many European Jews and early immigrants to the United States and Canada. Yiddish, a mixture of German, Slavic languages, and Hebrew, originated in the twelfth century in Germany. Every country

This road sign in Jerusalem is written in Hebrew, Arabic, and English.

in which the Jews lived also contributed words and pronunciations, but a French Jew speaking Yiddish can generally understand a Polish or Italian Jew speaking Yiddish.

Since Israel is a nation of immigrants, many other languages are spoken in the country. Arabic, one of the principal tongues of the world, is among the most widespread. It is used by Israeli Arabs both for prayer and for everyday life, and by workers who come into Israel from Jordan or the Palestinian-controlled territories. Jewish Israeli citizens of Arabic heritage also speak Arabic.

The influx of Russian immigrants into Israel in the early 1990s gave rise to the joke: "What is the second language of Israel?" The answer is Hebrew, implying that more people understand and speak Russian. Other Israelis speak Italian, Polish, Spanish, and African dialects. Almost everyone speaks English, which is a required subject in state schools.

Some visitors to Israel are surprised to see the numbers of young people in military uniform on the streets. Israel is in a state of constant military preparedness because of the potential for terrorist attacks. Soldiers, laden with packs and automatic weapons, hitchhike from designated stops on the main highways. Everyone over the age of 18 must serve in the military, except students attending the religious schools. Unmarried women serve two years of active duty and do not serve in combat roles, while men serve four years.

Even before Israel was a state, women guarded outposts and served in military units. Many women are instructors, teaching everything from sniping to tank maneuvers. Others

Both women and men are required to serve in the military.

help teach immigrant recruits from Ethiopia, Canada, India, England, France, and Morocco to speak, read, and write Hebrew.

Gradually, Israel is becoming more sure of itself as a nation, forged by the bravery and talents brought to it from many lands.

A Colorful Religious Mosaic

For good reason, Israel is considered "the Holy Land." Followers of three of the world's major religions—Jews, Muslims, and Christians—find their religious roots here. Several religious sects (groups of people having a common religion) such as the Druze and Baha'i also have centuries of connections here. Subsequently, Israel is a colorful spiritual mosaic. It almost seems as if every rock in the Holy Land has a spiritual significance to someone.

The Hebrew text on the building reads:
בית כנסת ע"ש רכה
THE HECHT SYNAGOGUE

Like almost every other aspect of life in the Middle East, nothing regarding religion is simple. An expression of religion is a political statement. Before Israel became an independent state, many countries jockeyed for power in the region. They used religion to gain a foothold for their own ambitions. As an example, Russia had authority over Greek and Russian Orthodox shrine sites in what was Palestine.

The Hecht Synagogue on the Mount of Olives in Jerusalem

Opposite: **A Greek Orthodox church on the Sea of Galilee**

The Roman Catholic Church of All Nations

France protected the monasteries of the Roman Catholic Church. Britain and Prussia (a country that later become part of Germany) kept watch over the few Protestant churches. Britain eventually extended its security umbrella over the Jews.

Religious Challenges

Since independence, Israelis have wrestled with challenges. They needed to merge a secular state with the religious traditions of a people whose centuries of survival had depended on their protecting their spiritual way of life. Subsequently, controversy is nothing new. Not only do representatives of the different religions in Israel often argue, but the Jewish religious minority and the nonreligious majority are at odds. Religious political parties often hold the balance of power in the Israeli government. And the question of "who is a Jew" is important. Today, under the country's Law of Return, a Jew automatically becomes a citizen when making his or her *aliyah* (immigration to Israel). But some ultra-Orthodox Jews want to limit the definition of who actually qualifies. They believe that Reform and Conservative Jews are not really Jews at all because they are not strict in their observance of all the religious laws.

Several Jewish groups refuse to recognize the state of Israel, emphasizing that a nation of God cannot be subordinated to secular law. As a result, there is always the potential for conflict when this wrangling is added to Israel's need to deal fairly with its Muslim and Christian citizens. Resolving such issues remains a formidable task for Israel's people and leaders, whether they attend religious services in a synagogue, a church, or a mosque, or do not attend them at all.

Jewish Groups Unite

When the newly formed State of Israel was defending itself against attacks by its Arab neighbors, Jews of every persuasion united to fight for their national sovereignty. Only a few diehards refused to assist. So cooperation among Jewish factions is possible.

Religions of Israel*	
Judaism	81%
Islam	15%
Christianity	3%
Druze	2%

*Does not equal 100% due to rounding

Compounding the mix of religious traditions has been the mass migration of Jews from dozens of countries to their spiritual homeland. *Sephardic* Jews came from Spain, the Middle East, and Africa, and the *Ashkenazim* came from Germany and Central and Eastern Europe. In 1984 and 1991, more than 21,000 Ethiopian Jews from Eastern Africa were airlifted to Israel. The African features of some immigrants contrast with those of the lighter-skinned European Jews. Others came from Yemen, on the Red Sea, and thousands more from North African countries such as Morocco. Early in the 1990s, almost 500,000 Russians arrived in Israel when the former Soviet Union collapsed. All these arrivals were eager to practice their faith openly and find new lives for themselves and their families.

Clothing Is Political

Articles of clothing hint at a Jew's political and religious persuasion. A *yarmulke* is a small cap worn by Orthodox and Conservative Jews during prayer. Some men wear yarmulkas at all times, even though the religious laws do not require it. A black cap is worn by more conservative Jews and a light-colored or white crocheted cap is worn by liberals. Even in the media, references are often made to disputes between the "Black Hats" and the "Crocheted Caps." This does not mean the bad guys versus the good guys as in old Western movies. It is just an easy way to identify the factions.

When praying, reverent Jewish men wear a *tallith*, a fringed, four-corned shawl. They then strap *tefillin*, black boxes containing writings from the Torah (Jewish law), to their hands and foreheads. This fulfills a biblical instruction that says, "You shall bind them as a sign on your hand and as frontlets between your eyes" (Deuteronomy 6:8).

The strict Orthodox communities are called *haredi* (God-fearing) and their members are *haredim*. Orthodox men wear a black coat, long sidelocks, and a black, broad-brimmed hat that is sometimes trimmed with fur. This shows that they are separate from the world. Women always keep their heads covered.

Jerusalem's Mea Shearim is one haredi neighborhood. Central to the lifestyle there are the *yeshivot* (religious schools) where pupils study the Torah. A single school is a *yeshiva*.

Jewish children at the Western Wall

The students also read the Talmud, a collection of Jewish laws, traditions, and writings. From the age of four until marriage, and often long afterward, male haredim spend most of their day poring over these verses. A yeshiva is not a quiet place. Arguments over the meaning and interpretations of the Scriptures are part of the learning process. The students loudly repeat the lessons chanted by their teachers. Yeshiva students are exempt from serving in the military.

A collection of Torahs

In the mid-1990s, there were some 50,000 yeshiva students. The number is growing because there is a large birthrate in haredi families. Ten or more children are not uncommon because haredim take to heart the biblical passage to "be fruitful and multiply." The government also awards study grants for yeshiva students. The families place a high value on study. Fathers are always pleased to marry their daughters to scholars.

Pilgrims at the Wailing Wall

The holiest place for Jews in Israel is the remains of the Western Wall of the Temple in Jerusalem, most of which was destroyed by the Romans in A.D. 70. Held by Jordan from 1948 to 1967, the wall was retaken by Israeli paratroopers in the Six-Day War. Soldiers swear an oath of allegiance to Israel during ceremonies there, with rifles and machine guns lined up alongside prayer books.

Sometimes called the "Wailing Wall," the Western Wall attracts tens of thousands of pilgrims every year. There, they chant the *kinot* (dirges) and lament the fall of Jerusalem and loss of the Temple. A *mechitsah*, a barricade outside in the wide courtyard fronting the wall, separates praying Orthodox men from women. The wall is a popular spot for *bar mitzvahs*, Jewish ceremonies in which a boy passes into manhood. (The ceremonies for girls are *bat mitzvahs*.) All guests must cover their heads when they visit the site.

A Jewish soldier praying at the Western Wall

The Jewish Sabbath and religious festivals are strictly observed in Israel. Most shops, factories, farms, offices, and restaurants close and public transportation halts from sundown Friday to sunset Saturday. However, taxis still operate and private cars crowd the roads. Soccer matches are played and crowds head to the beach or to a park for a picnic. This irritates some of the more Orthodox Jews, who think the day should be reserved for religious activities.

"Leshanah tovah tikatevu," ("May you be inscribed for a Happy New Year") is a blessing heard in every Jewish home around the world on *Rosh Hashanah* (the Jewish New

Year). Other celebrations include *Yom Kippur* (the Day of Atonement) and *Purim*, commemorating the biblical figure Esther's deliverance of her people from a massacre by Haman, a courtier of her husband, King Ahasuerus. Passover marks the exodus of the Jewish slaves from Egypt. An end-of-harvest festival is called the Feast of Sukkot.

Jews celebrating Sukkot in Jerusalem

Overseeing the various Jewish communities are the rabbis, or *rebbes* (ordained teachers of Jewish law), who meet in councils to discuss issues of the day. The heads of some groups live abroad. The late Lubbavicher Rebbe Menachem Mendel Schneersohn, for instance, lived in Brooklyn, New York. In Israel, his followers built a replica of his U.S. apartment house.

Muslims Submit to God

The word *Islam* means "submission to God" in Arabic. A person who "submits" belongs to the faith of Islam. Its followers are called Muslims. Muslims make up about 15 percent of the Israeli population. They follow the teachings outlined in the Koran, their holy book, which is their guide to everything in life. It is believed the Koran's contents were revealed to the prophet Muhammad by God, or *Allah* in Arabic.

Muhammad lived in the Arabian town of Mecca. He objected to the paganism of people around him, but few people listened to him so he and his followers were chased away into the desert. This is called "the flight," or the *hegira*, which marks the beginning of the Muslim calendar. According to the Gregorian calendar we follow in North America, this took place in the year A.D. 622.

Muhammad organized an army and soon defeated his enemies. Muslim forces eventually swept through the entire Middle East, much of Africa, and into Southern Europe and Asia. Before a battle, they would shout, "There is no god but Allah and Muhammad is His prophet." Muslims around the world today proclaim this belief daily.

Some of the mosques in today's Israel were once Christian churches, captured by the Muslim armies. Europe's Crusaders of the Middle Ages intended to drive the Muslims out of the Holy Land but were only partly successful. Ruins of Crusader castles still dot the Israeli landscape.

Old Traditions Followed

Muslims follow centuries-old traditions. In addition to proclaiming their belief, the faithful pray five times daily, facing in the direction of Mecca. Traditionally, muezzins (criers) stood on a balcony high atop a minaret (a tower attached to a mosque) to call the faithful to prayer. Today, a recording is often played from the minaret instead. Other duties of Muslims include giving alms to the poor, and fasting (eating very little or nothing) during Ramadan, the ninth month of the Muslim year. During Ramadam, Muslims fast between sunrise and sunset. A big feast marks the welcome end of the fasting. At least once in their lives, devout Muslims who can afford it must make a pilgrimage to the holy city of Mecca.

Friday is the Muslim holy day, when Muslims do not work. This is not a problem in Israel because Muslim holy days and festivals are officially recognized by the state. The Arabic station on the Israel Broadcasting Authority airs daily readings from the Koran, as well as sermons on Fridays.

Many of today's problems in Israel stem from an age-old mistrust between Jews and Muslims. Just before and after Palestine became the State of Israel, many Palestinian

Muslim men praying in Hebron

Muslims fled to other Arab countries, and others remained in the sprawling refugee camps in the Gaza Strip along the Mediterranean Sea.

In an effort to help those who stayed in Israel, Israel's Ministry of Religious Affairs reestablished Muslim institutions. It also rebuilt mosques damaged in the numerous wars between Israel and its Arab neighbors. However, the Palestinian refugees wanted land that was taken during the various conflicts to be returned. Compounding this problem, Jewish settlers have built settlements in parts of the disputed

The Dome of the Rock

Jerusalem's Dome of the Rock, one of the holiest shrines in Islam, is easy to identify. Much photographed, it glows in the sun and dramatically stands out against the city's other buildings. In 1994, Jordan's King Hussein donated 176 pounds (80 kg) of gold to recoat the surface of the dome. The building was constructed in the seventh century by Caliph Abd el-Malik to enclose a shrine to Muhammad. Here it is said that the prophet Abraham offered his son Isaac for sacrifice. It was from this rock that Muhammad is believed to have ascended to heaven. One of the best places to view the dome is from the Haas Promenade on the Mount of Olives. This observation site is across a valley from the Old City, just above an ancient Jewish cemetery.

territory. Ongoing talks between the Israeli government and the Palestinian Authority, which governs Palestinian lands, are attempting to resolve this conflict.

A Volatile Mix of Values

This volatile mix of land issues, religious fervor, mistrust, and outright hatred has led to a spiral of violence. Muslim suicide bombers blow up a bus on a Tel Aviv street. An ultra-Orthodox Jewish soldier shoots Muslims at prayer. Jewish and Muslim children throw stones at one another. Yet despite the dangers, peace groups on both sides attempt to bring their communities together. After all, they say, we should respect each other because we have the same religious roots.

Israeli Druze

The Israeli Druze are Arabic speakers who follow a secretive religion that broke from Islam almost a thousand years ago. The Druze name is derived from that of al-Darazi, one of its founders. The Druze believe that souls pass from one body to another after death. They also believe Caliph al-Hakim bi'Amr Allah to be the messiah (savior). This religious leader mysteriously disappeared in 1021 in Egypt. The basic doctrines in the Druze religion are understood by only a few select leaders of the community and are not shared with the community at large. A small museum in the Druze village of Daliat el Carmel proudly displays artifacts of their culture. To become a Druze, a person must be born into the community, and no converts have been accepted by the Druze since 1034.

The Druze have few ceremonies or rituals but make pilgrimages to the grave of Jethro, Moses' father-in-law, which is near Karnei-Hittim in Galilee. The hospitable Druze have easily blended in with the rest of Israeli society and openly share their homes and food with visitors. Noted for their fighting abilities, many Druze achieve officer rank in the army and border patrol.

A Holy Tomb

The Baha'i faith is named after its founder, *Baha Allah* ("The Splendor of God"). His tomb near Acre ('Akko) is considered

The Baha'i gardens in Haifa

the holiest place on earth. Baha'i developed out of a Muslim mystical movement that arose in Persia (now Iran) during the 1840s. The promotion of unity among all people and encouragement of equal rights for men and women are among Baha'i tenets, or laws.

The Baha'i international center is the sprawling Baha'i Shrine in Haifa, completed in 1953. Expansive gardens of towering cedar and spruce trees and winding walks beautify the grounds. The Baha'i were glad to see Zionist Jews moving back to Israel at the end of the nineteenth century. They felt that this was foretold in the writings of their spiritual leaders. The Baha'i were among the first non-Jews to recognize the new State of Israel.

Almost every principal branch of Christianity is represented in Israel. The most ancient Christian group is the Greek Orthodox Church, established in the Holy Land as early as the second century after Jesus Christ's death. It is the only Christian religious community headquartered in today's Israel. Other Christian groups with extensive Holy Land connections are based elsewhere. For instance, Vatican City in Rome, Italy, is the religious center for Roman Catholics even though there are many Catholic churches and shrines in Israel.

Russian and Syrian Orthodox, Armenian, and numerous other Christian sects are also present. The Catholics have more than forty-five religious orders and congregations, including the Salesians, Benedictines, Franciscans, Dominicans, and Carmelites. In addition, there are thirty communities of nuns, each with its own convent. The Uniates, a sect linked with the Roman Catholic Church, live mainly along the border with Lebanon. Finally, there are Episcopalians, Lutherans, and other Protestant Christians.

A group of nuns in Jerusalem

Small Communities Abound

Numerous smaller communities also live in Israel. And the different groups do not always get along well. Ethiopian monks live atop Jerusalem's Church of the Holy Sepulchre, one of Christianity's holiest shrines. The church was built on the cliffside where Jesus Christ was said to be buried. Generations ago, the monks were restricted to the roof after a long-running and often bloody feud with Coptic Christians over who managed the church and collected donations. Despite these odd living arrangements, the Ethiopians claim a pre-Christian link to the city. For centuries, the emperors of Ethiopia, an eastern African nation, have been called the "Lions of Judah."

Israel is also home to a group of Black Hebrews, a non-Jewish religious community whose members come from Atlanta, Chicago, Washington, and other U.S. cities. Although they are not Israeli citizens, the government settled them in the Negev city of Dimona. They maintain their own schools, social institutions, and gardens.

The Samaritans are an independent people who trace their origins far back into the Scriptures. They lived in the Holy Land at least two thousand years before the birth of Jesus. They believe that Moses is the sole prophet of God. Samaritans also expect that a "restorer" will return on the Last Day of Earth and lead his chosen people, including the Samaritans, to paradise.

Karaites recognize the Scripture as the only direct source of religious law. Over centuries, they evolved from a mix of traditions derived from Jews living in ancient Persia and from Arab and other Middle Eastern cultures.

Arts and Sports across Ethnic Lines

Israel's wonderful mixture of cultures has enhanced its arts, entertainment, and sports. Every nationality, religious system, and political creed that makes up the Israeli scene brings a talent or creative thought to share. Sometimes this causes interesting dilemmas.

The Israel Philharmonic
Orchestra

To ENSURE THAT EVERYONE GETS A "PIECE OF THE ACTION," Jerusalem city councilman Yehoram Gaon is responsible for funding arts groups in his city. In addition to being an elected official, Gaon is one of Israel's leading actors and singers. Gaon laughs that he needs detective abilities to sort out the needs of the various groups he services. Demonstrating that religion plays a part in every aspect of Israeli life, Gaon once secured funding for a choir of Orthodox Jewish women. However, he could not go to its shows because the women were not allowed to perform in front of men.

Arts Are Open

Generally, the arts are open to anyone. Yet challenges remain. Many Israeli writers are unknown outside Israel, partly

Opposite: **Dancing at an outdoor celebration**

because Hebrew is not widely spoken outside the country. Even many Israelis admit that they don't know the language well. Shmuel Yosef Agnon (1888-1970), the only Israeli to win a Nobel Prize for Literature, often wrote in German because he grew up in Germany. Agnon, who moved to Israel in 1913, won the world's most prestigious writing award in 1966. His novels and short stories about Jewish life combine social satire with religious and mystical themes. Among his best-known works are *A Simple Story* (1935), *The Bridal Canopy* (1937), and *Only Yesterday* (1945).

But the word is getting out about the quality of Israel's literary scene. Poet Arnon Levy, born in Jerusalem in 1975, read his works at a seminar of young poets at the Rotterdam Poetry Festival in The Netherlands in 1997. Yehuda Amichai has composed eleven volumes of poetry since 1956, all of which have been translated from Hebrew into many languages, including Chinese and Japanese. In his poem "National Thoughts," Amichai writes about how his native language "was torn from its sleep in the Bible" to became a contemporary language.

Writers

Zbigniew Herbert from Poland, Vasko Popa from the former Yugoslavia, Andrei Voznesensky from the former Soviet Union, and Robert Friend from the United States are other writers now proud to be Israelis. They write in Hebrew, as well as in their native tongue. Phillip Hyams is typical of the new breed of Israeli literary figures who came from abroad. He was born in 1959, in Tétouan, Morocco, and came to Israel with his parents in 1972. His book of poems entitled *Litany of the Immigrant* has heartfelt interpretations of a newcomer's feelings about Israel.

Israel's many adopted literary sons and daughters can be added to its home-born talent. Among the younger native writers are Salman Mashalah, born in 1953 in the Druze town of M'gar in central Galilee, and Sharon Ahsse, born in Ramat Gan in 1966.

To help spread the word about Israel's literary community, the government started *Ariel*, a quarterly literary magazine. Essays, short stories, poems, reviews, and personality profiles overflow its pages. *Ariel* is published in English, French, German, Russian, Spanish, and Arabic. It even has its own Internet page and e-mail connections.

Importance of Music

Music has always been important to the Israelis. Israeli pop songwriters regularly place high among the top winners of the annual Euro Music competition. On the more classical side, the Israel Philharmonic Orchestra is internationally known for its sweeping sounds and impressive presentations. Noted guest

Violinist Yitzhak Perlman was born in Israel.

musicians such as violinist Yitzhak Perlman and pianist/conductor Daniel Barenboim, both Israelis, regularly appear at its concerts. The orchestra plays in the 3,000-seat Mann Auditorium in Tel Aviv, the country's largest performance hall. The orchestra also regularly presents outdoor concerts in the Yarkon Park at the northern end of that modern city.

Each year, the Leonard Bernstein International Music Competition is held in Jerusalem. This is a cycle of three competitions. In 1995, the first award was given for conducting an orchestra. In 1996, honors went for classical singing. The 1997 award was given in composing. The orchestral works are performed by the Jerusalem Symphony Orchestra under the direction of Mendi Rodan. The competition promotes artistic causes supported by Bernstein, a noted New York-based musician, composer, and conductor.

Bernstein especially wanted to help young performers. The municipality of Jerusalem, the Jerusalem Foundation, and Bernstein's estate decided that the contest would be a fine way to honor his memory and his support of the arts. This competition is only one of several hosted by Israeli arts groups. The Pablo Casals Cello Competition is another. That contest honors the great Spanish musician, who was born in 1876 and died in 1973.

Israelis Like Popular Music

Israelis like other forms of music, especially jazz. The Red Sea Jazz Festival is held each year in Eilat. New York jazz artists appeared in the courtyard of the Tower of David Museum in Jerusalem in late 1997. Trumpeter Marlon Jordon, pianist Eric Reed, drummer Louis Hayes, and other stars performed under the stars. As floodlights illuminated the harsh stone walls of the old fort, concertgoers perched on every open space to listen.

Rock and roll is of course popular with young Israelis. In addition to listening to visiting international stars, they like the sounds of local heroes such as Johnny Blista and VJ Vadim. Nightclubs in Tel Aviv stay open until the early hours of the morning. Thundering music by Gemini Cricket, Wow Mom, D.J. Adi Lev, and Lipstik Sing has everyone dancing. Flashing strobe lights blast the interior of the clubs with brilliant explosions of red, green, and white. Smoke from dry ice fills the rooms, almost hiding the bands onstage. The loud, throbbing beat guarantees that no one will sit still for long.

On a lower decibel count, Tel Aviv's Golda Meir Performing Arts Center is one of the country's premier halls. It was built 1994. Operas such as *Seven Deadly Sins* and *Kaiser of Atlantis* have been staged there.

More traditional fare is also popular. *Klezmer* instrumental music started in Eastern Europe during the seventeenth century. Its distinctive mix of drums, violins, and clarinets along with keyboard and tambourines is played at weddings and

The Feld dance troupe

at *bar* and *bat mitzvahs*. In the late 1990s, four young women formed Eve's Daughters, a high-powered klezmer band that packs the country's clubs and concert halls.

> ### Dance

Professional Israeli dancers are internationally known for their form, creativity, and style. The Israel Ballet Company is well received wherever it appears. Inbal, Batsheeva, and Bat Dor are the most

A Rising Star of Dance

Ido Tadmor, one of the rising young stars of Israeli dance, was born in Jerusalem in 1964. Tadmor danced for several of the country's major troupes before being invited to join the Lar Lubovitch Dance Company of New York in 1990. He performed at the Lincoln Center for the Performing Arts and at the Jacob's Pillow Festival in Beckett, Massachusetts. He founded his own company in 1995. Tadmor has performed at the prestigious Tokyo Festival for Contemporary Dance.

popular modern dance troupes. Choreographers and producers such as Ohad Nahrin are known everywhere. In addition to the large troupes, numerous smaller companies are continually forming, dancing, merging, and fading as young performers move from production to production.

Several kibbutzim have dance companies that give young dancers their first performance opportunities. Uri Ivgi was raised on Kibbutz Hulta and began dancing there in 1990. In 1994, he was awarded first prize as best dancer at the Suzanne Dellal International Dance Competition in Tel Aviv. The competition is sponsored by the Suzanne Dellal Centre for Dance and Theatre, which brings the best dancers and companies together. The Dellal Centre is hidden away in a corner of Neve Tzedek, one of Tel Aviv's oldest neighborhoods. Every day, eager students flock here to see their country's top performers practice.

A well-known folk dance is the *hora*. This exuberant dance, with its intricate steps, is enjoyed by all Israelis regardless of their age. It is exciting to do any time.

Theater Classics

Amalia Eyal, who works at Haifa Repertory Theater, says Israel is the "paradise of theater." The Arab Theater and the others are constantly packed. Noted actors such as Shimon Israely and actresses like Gila Almagor are in demand. Israelis love the theater because of the harsh political reality that surrounds them. Theater is the art of escape.

Israelis love dramatic classics, such as Isaac Bashevis Singer's *Teibele & Her Demon*. Other plays touch on the current Palestine-Israel conflict, the peace talks, and similar contemporary issues facing the many ethnic and religious communities in Israel. Most plays are produced in Hebrew, but there are now Russian theater companies and groups representing other nationalities. Many playhouses offer English translations through headsets.

The Jerusalem Film Center, with its archives, library, and viewings, also brings together Israelis of various backgrounds. The center's Jerusalem Film Festival annually features more than 150 films. Israeli filmmakers are proficient in making documentary movies, which feature incidents from life. Yaakov Gross and his *Pioneers of Zion* (1995) and Ruth Beckermann's *Toward Jerusalem* (1992) are two such award-winning pieces.

The country's media give a lot of exposure to the arts community. Rivka Michaeli hosts entertainment personalities on

Asim Abu-Shakra

Asim Abu-Shakra (1961–1990) was a young Arab Israeli painter whose work was widely exhibited around the country. One of his main themes was the cactus, which he drew in many shapes and positions. Some critics considered his modernistic work a metaphor—a figure of speech that compares one thing to another—for his life as a Muslim living in a primarily Jewish community. In his short career, Abu-Shakra is credited with raising his country's consciousness about the position of the Arab in Israeli society.

her televised morning show. She is called the "Oprah Winfrey of Israel" because her program is similar to that of the popular talk-show host in the United States. On the print side, David Isaacson, editor of the arts and entertainment section of the *Jerusalem Post* newspaper, often spotlights new performers.

There is a great flowering of painting and sculpture in Israel. The Museum of Contemporary Art in Tel Aviv and the Israel Museum in Jerusalem have some of the most extensive art collections in the world. Jewish benefactors from many countries have donated their personal collections, as well as money, to fill the country's largest museums. There are also numerous private galleries, such as the Ilana Goor Museum and Gallery, which stands in a narrow alley in the ancient seaport of Jaffa. The museum, gallery, and theater complex of Bet Gavriel in Tiberias hosted high-level Israeli-Palestinian peace talks. Participants worked out their differences in a conference room there, overlooking the shores of the Sea of Galilee.

Artists at work at the village of Ein Hod

Visual Arts

Zelig Segal proudly shows his intricate metalwork in a shop in Jerusalem's Designer Quarter, near the Old City's Jaffa Gate. Designer Sam Phillipe displays his statuary in major hotels. Both specialize in Judaica, artistic renditions of items of worship or pieces with Jewish themes. An entire colony of artists lives at Ein

Hod, a colorful village south of Haifa. The Mediterranean Sea's soft breeze brushes the wind chimes hanging from porches and rustles colorful pennants draped from tree branches. Raya Zommer manages the village's Janco Dada gallery. A whimsical display by one of her artists featured live chickens! Another showcased "clothing" made of wire mesh.

Sports

Israelis love sports of all kinds. They bowl, swim, parasail, climb mountains, ride horses, fish, race motorcycles and kayaks, shoot pool, and play card games such as bridge. Whitewater rafting on the Jordan River; rappelling, or

Whitewater rafting on the Jordan River

Rock climbers practice rappelling in the Negev Desert.

Israel *(left)* plays Cyprus in the 1997 World Cup qualifier.

climbing with ropes, down cliffs in the Negev Desert; off-road four-wheel driving; and dirt-bike riding also have their fans. Rugby clubs such as ASA Tel Aviv and Rishon Lezion XV regularly battle for national championships.

The most popular team sports are soccer and basketball. Israel's national soccer team is one of the strongest in the Middle East. Coach Shlomo Scharf has a good eye for recruiting top players. Scharf's squad hopes to play in the European Nations Championship, to be held in Belgium and The Netherlands in the year 2000.

National Titles

The powerhouse of the Israeli Basketball League is Maccabi Tel Aviv, which has won 38 national titles since World War II. It captured 23 consecutive championships from 1970 to 1992, when the streak was broken by the skilled players of Hapoel Gailil Elyon, led by American-born guard Brad Leaf. But

Ken Barlow sinks a basket for Maccabi in Moscow.

The World Maccabiah Games

The World Maccabiah Games are the Jewish Olympics. The games started in 1932 and have been held every four years since then in the year following the Olympic Summer Games. The string of competitions was interrupted only during World War II.

Jewish athletes come to Israel from around the world to participate. Among the best was swimmer Mark Spitz of the United States—a five-time gold medal winner in the Olympics. Athletes are lodged with others in the same sport, rather than by nationality.

The games include swimming, wrestling, rowing, squash, bowling, track and field, softball, gymnastics, and other sports. Encouraged by Canadians, ice hockey was even placed on the venue. Not too surprisingly, the tough Canadian national team then took the gold medal in 1997. The Israeli ice hockey team at that time consisted of players from Russia, Canada, and the United States. Ron Oz, a young soldier from Tel Aviv, was the only native-born Israeli. Demonstrating the internationalism of the games, the hockey team was coached by Jacques Demers, a French-Canadian Catholic.

Maccabi had already won the European basketball championships in 1977 and 1980. The most important game for Maccabi was its upset of CSKA Moscow, the Soviet Army team, during the 1977 tournament. The Israelis defeated the Soviets, 91-79. The game's Israeli hero was Tal Brody, a former all-American from the University of Illinois. He was recruited to play for Israel by coach Noah Klieger, a Frenchman who survived the Auschwitz concentration camp. The basketball league even has its own Web page on the Internet.

Israel sent three Russian-born ice skaters to the 1998 Winter Olympics in Japan. Figure skater Misha Shmerkin was in his second Olympic go-around for Israel, and ice-dance couple Galit Chait and Sergei Sakanovsky were in their first Olympics. Chait and Sakanovsky trained in Delaware before they left for the games. Shmerkin practiced at the ice rink at Metulla, in northern Israel, which is becoming the country's major sports training center. The Olympic-sized facility was built by donations from the Canadian Jewish community. The skaters did well but did not place in the top ranks.

Other Israelis have also won Olympic medals. Yachtsman Gal Fridman was the only Israeli citizen to capture a medal at the 1996 Summer Olympic Games in Atlanta, Georgia. He took the bronze. As a sailor, it is appropriate that his first name translates to "wave." Israel's first Olympic winners were judo experts Yael Arad and Oren Smadja, who earned the silver and bronze respectively at the 1992 Barcelona games.

Yael Arad won a silver medal at the 1992 Olympic Games in Barcelona.

Since 1982, thousands of runners have converged on the shores of the Dead Sea for a marathon. The 13-mile (21-km) race attracts runners from age twelve and up. Events start the night before the race with a dinner at the Kibbutz Ein Gedi, home of an open-air botanical garden.

A Young Gymnastics Champ

Olga Menin became Israel's junior gymnastics champion in 1995, when she was only twelve years old. She is already working hard to qualify for the Olympic Games to be held in Sydney, Australia, in the year 2000. Menin began her training in Russia when she was five years old, coming to Israel with her family when she was seven. In 1997, she came alone to Boston, Massachusetts, to receive additional training. She lives in her coach's house along with other young gymnasts. Throughout the week, she studies, trains, does homework, and then has more workouts. On the Sabbath, she admits, she sleeps a great deal.

The Cousins Are Coming

Aaron Hoffmann can hardly control his excitement. Any minute now, he expects to see Aunt Lisa and Uncle Chaim and his cousins, Josef, David, and Rachel, driving down the street in their four-wheel-drive truck. They are coming for a week's visit. To get a better view, Aaron perches on a chair, looking out of an upper-front window.

A

Return from Minnesota

ARON'S FAMILY HAS JUST RETURNED FROM A YEAR IN St. Paul, Minnesota, where his father, Ben, taught Middle Eastern art history at the University of Minnesota. He is now lecturing at the Hebrew University in Jerusalem, a short drive from their home. Aaron's mother, Ruth, is a sculptor. Several of her works are on display at the Jerusalem Artists' House on Shmuel Hanagid Street and at the Safrai gallery on King David Street.

While waiting for his cousins, Aaron looks at a picture on the wall. It shows Uncle Chaim and his father with their arms around each other's shoulders. They are brothers, proudly wearing their army uniforms. Next to that picture is a photo of Grandpa and Grandma Hoffmann. In 1956, they came from South Africa to Haifa, where they still live. Then there is a photo of Grandpa and Grandma Elazar, his mom's father and mother. They were born when Israel was still called Palestine, and they lived on a kibbutz near the Jordan River after they were married. Aaron never met them. They died many years ago when a rocket hit their home during one of the wars Israel had with its Arab neighbors. Aaron's mother and her three sisters were working in Tel Aviv at the time and escaped injury. Aaron knows his mother and aunts still miss their parents, especially during holidays. His aunts now have large families, so Aaron has about a dozen other cousins living in Israel, in addition to Josef, David, and Rachel.

Opposite: **Visiting the Israel Museum**

Ein Kerem is a town rich in religious history.

Move to Ein Kerem

Aaron and his folks live in Ein Kerem, a neighborhood on the western heights of Jerusalem. Off to the left, above the nearby houses, Aaron can just see the top of a tower built above the Spring of the Virgin. His dad says that Mary, the mother of Jesus, supposedly drank water there. Although his family is Jewish, Aaron knows a lot about the Christian faith. Many of his friends back in the United States were Christian. He uses e-mail to keep in touch with them.

Home to Churches

Ein Kerem used to be an Arab village, one abandoned to Jewish settlers after Israel gained its independence in 1948. Jerusalem eventually expanded to surround the neat, tidy neighborhood. Ein Kerem is the home of several ancient Christian churches that have remained tourist attractions. Aaron is used to seeing motor coaches stopping outside the Franciscan Church of St. John the Baptist, the Catholic Church of the Visitation, and the Russian Church. The sites are noted in guidebooks. Most of the visitors are older people. They always take a lot of pictures. One time, a woman from Canada took Aaron's photograph when he was walking past the Church of St. John the Baptist. Aaron was on his way to a soccer match when she asked if she could take his photo. Aaron was surprised when the woman's husband even gave him a shekel! On his way home, Aaron bought a *gazoz*, a fruit-flavored drink, and then put the change in a special box he uses for his vacation savings.

Dietary Laws

According to religious law, Orthodox Jews are not allowed to light fires on Saturday, the Sabbath. Hot food can be prepared the day before the Sabbath and then placed in a hot oven overnight. *Cholent*, a stew made with beans, potatoes, rice, and meat, is a popular Sabbath meal that is easy to prepare in that manner. Jews from North Africa add an extra twist by placing eggs on top of the stew. The eggs become hard-boiled as the stew cooks. A salad made with red and green peppers is served as a delicious side dish, along with plenty of fresh fruit. Also under kosher laws, separate eating utensils must be used for meat and dairy dishes.

As the heat of mid-morning increases, the summer air becomes rich with a perfume from the rosebushes outside Aaron's front door. The blue sky overhead seems never to end.

Friends

Aaron waves to Noah and Sammy, two of his school buddies who live down the road. They are outside talking with Asim, whose father is one of Israel's up-and-coming young Arab artists. They are ready to play soccer. Aaron and Asim favor Hapoel Jerusalem, the local professional team. Sammy likes Betar Jerusalem, and Noah roots for Hapoel Tel Aviv because he was born there. Aaron's bedroom is papered with posters and photos of his favorite players.

Arab boys practice with a soccer ball in the streets of Jerusalem's Old City.

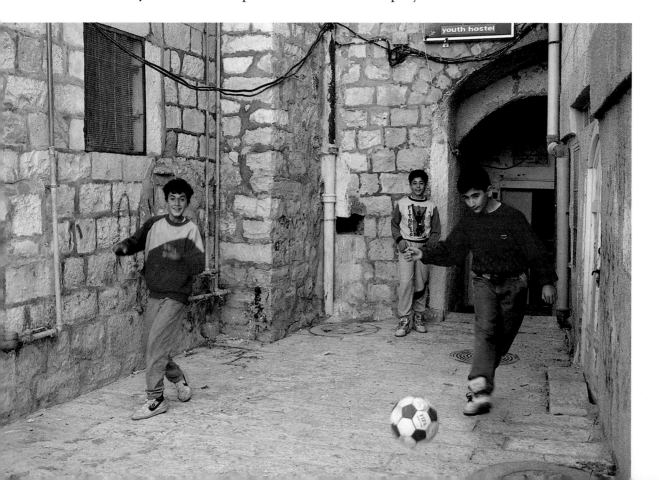

A lot of other painters, actors, and television personalities also live in Ein Kerem, a mixed area of Jewish, Muslim, and Christian professionals. Aaron's mom and dad know many of them through their work in the arts community.

Life on a Kibbutz

Uncle Chaim, Aunt Lisa, and their children live on a kibbutz in the Judean hills, where Chaim runs a tour service in the desert high above the Dead Sea. Aunt Lisa is a nurse on the kibbutz, a communal farm not far from the mountain fortress of Masada. Almost two thousand years ago, Jewish fighters killed themselves there rather than surrender to a Roman army. It is one of the most famous historical sites in Israel. Two years ago, Aaron spent a week with his cousins on the kibbutz. Uncle Chaim took everyone to Masada and they rode a cable car up the mountainside.

The cable car to Masada

Jerusalem doesn't have a cable car but there is plenty to do. The first thing Aaron plans to do is take his cousins to the soccer pitch near Hadassah Hospital, where there is a funny-looking sculpture designed by Niki de Saint Phalle. The statue is a silly monster with each of its three tongues used as a slide by all the little kids who live nearby. Aaron's dad once took him inside Hadassah Hospital to show him the stained-glass windows there. They were designed by the famous artist Marc Chagall. If they have time between kicking the soccer ball, Aaron will probably show his cousins the famous windows. He is sure they will be impressed.

According to the plan, Uncle Chaim and Aunt Lisa will drop off their children and drive home. Then, after the cousins' weeklong holiday in Jerusalem, Aaron's parents will take everyone back to the Ein Gedi kibbutz on the western rim of the Dead Sea, where the cousins live. The kibbutz is close to the Ein Gedi Nature Reserve, where Uncle Chaim often takes his tourist guests. Ein Gedi also has a beach and a tourist resort. Both families plan on playing at Ein Gedi for a day. Aaron and his cousins have their heart set on splashing in the huge, outdoor swimming pool, and their parents are eager to have massages and take the mud treatments.

Israel's Official Holidays

The Jewish calendar has fewer days each year than the Gregorian calendar used in the United States and Canada, so specific Western dates of holidays vary each year.

New Year of Trees	January–February
Purim	March
Passover	April
Holocaust Memorial Day	April–May
Memorial Day	April–May
Independence Day	April–May
Lag Ba'Omer	April–May
Jerusalem Day	May–June
Shavuot (Pentecost)	May–June
Tisha B'Av	July–August
Rosh Hashana	September–October
Yom Kippur	September–October
Sukkot	September–October
Simchat Torah	October
Hanukkah	December

National Day is celebrated in November by the Palestinian Authority in the West Bank and the Gaza Strip. Ramadan is the most important Muslim holy season, when Muslims fast for an entire month. The Muslim calendar year is shorter by two weeks than the Gregorian calendar year, so Ramadan is held on different Western dates each year.

Used to Urban Life

Aaron is used to a city's hustle and bustle. He doesn't mind the rushing traffic and loves the international flavor. Even though he is only in sixth grade, Aaron

speaks English, Hebrew, and French and wants to study another language. Right now, he is thinking about a job with the Israeli foreign service after his university studies so he can travel some more. But that is a long way in the future.

Getting away for that week in the desert with his cousins was especially fun. He saw a gazelle, rode a camel, and bounced across the desert trails on his uncle's all-terrain vehicle. Now it is his turn to show off his city. Aaron and his folks have already worked out an itinerary. They are going to the Israel Museum, of course, where the kids' section has plenty of hands-on activities. The flashy, modern Jerusalem Mall, the largest shopping center in the Middle East, is also on the list. It is near the Teddy Kollek soccer stadium, one of Aaron's favorite places. The stadium is named after a popular long-time mayor of Jerusalem.

The Jerusalem Mall is the largest shopping mall in the Middle East.

Scouts for Peace

The Hebrew Scouts are the Jewish segment of the Israeli scouting network. There are also units for Muslims and Christians. The Religious Scouts and the Sea Scouts are part of the Hebrew Scouts. The Hebrew Scout Association is divided into eight regions, with "tribes" in each region consisting of 50 to 2,000 members. The tribes are broken into units called patrols.

The Israeli scouting system is based on ages corresponding to the grade in school. At the beginning of every year, each patrol moves from one age level to the next. Up to age fourteen, boys and girls are in separate patrols. Then they merge into a mixed senior unit to which they can belong for four years.

Scouts from Israel and Jordan released doves beneath a "peace" banner on the King Hussein Bridge when the second border crossing between the two countries opened in 1994.

Balance Old and New

To balance the new with the old, Aaron and his cousins are also going to walk through the narrow alleys of the Old City. Their mothers enjoy poking around the small shops and stalls, driving hard bargains when they see something they want.

As he continues watching out the window, a wonderful new aroma tickles Aaron's nose. His mom is preparing a great stack of snacks, knowing that everyone will be really hungry after their long car ride. She is baking *zalabi*, a buttered fritter sprinkled with brown sugar. Already on the kitchen table is a delicious honey cake, with an interesting mix of instant coffee, raisins, cloves, lemon peel, and all sorts of other ingredients. A porcelain bowl overflowing with ripe apples, bananas, oranges, dates, and kiwi fruit rests on one side of the table. The only things missing are pomegranates, lusciously juicy pink fruit with tiny seeds that snap when eaten. Aunt Lisa always brings extra pomegranates from their kibbutz. Aaron thinks they are the best in the world.

At last Aaron hears the rumble of an engine from down the street. A large black truck with passenger seats boldly rounds the corner at the top of the hill, driven by a fellow with a great red beard. It's Uncle Chaim! "Hoffmann's Desert Tours" is splashed across both sides of his vehicle. The bright green lettering swirls around a picture of a galloping ibex. Assorted cousins hang out of every window. Chaim honks the horn and waves when he sees Aaron.

"They're here! They're here," Aaron yells down to his folks. He hits the stairs running. It's time to see Jerusalem!

Timeline

History of Israel

Semitic Amorite clans populate Canaan (Israel).	3000– 2000 B.C.
Israelites conquer Jericho and occupy much of today's Israel.	1020– 1004
Alexander the Great conquers Israel.	332
Egyptian king Ptolemy captures Jerusalem.	312– 199
The Romans capture Jerusalem.	63
Jesus is crucified.	c. A.D. 25
Jerusalem is destroyed by the Romans.	70
Jewish rebels die at Masada.	73
Helena, the mother of Emperor Constantine, comes to Jerusalem and begins repairing the holy sites.	326
The prophet Muhammad is born in Medina.	570
The Arabs capture Palestine.	638
The Crusaders capture Jerusalem.	1099
Saladin, Kurdish sultan of Egypt, captures Jerusalem.	1187
Franciscan monks settle in Jerusalem.	1334

World History

c. 2500 B.C.	Egyptians build the Pyramids and Sphinx in Giza.
563 B.C.	Buddha is born in India.
A.D. 313	The Roman emperor Constantine recognizes Christianity.
610	The prophet Muhammad begins preaching a new religion called Islam.
1054	The Eastern (Orthodox) and Western (Roman) Churches break apart.
1066	William the Conqueror defeats the English in the Battle of Hastings.
1095	Pope Urban II proclaims the First Crusade.
1215	King John seals the Magna Carta.
1300s	The Renaissance begins in Italy.
1347	The Black Death sweeps through Europe.
1453	Ottoman Turks capture Constantinople, conquering the Byzantine Empire.

History of Israel

French ruler Napoleon I fails to capture the Holy Land.	1799
Earthquake devastates the Holy Land.	1837
Eliezer Ben-Yehuda brings Hebrew to Palestine as a national language.	1881
The first kibbutz is founded at Degania near the Sea of Galilee.	1909
Hebrew University is founded on Jerusalem's Mount Scopus.	1925
As Hitler comes to power in Germany, German Jews flee to Palestine.	1933–1938
More than 6 million Jews are murdered during the Nazi Holocaust.	1939–1945
The state of Israel is declared by David Ben-Gurion on May 14.	1948
Israel wars with Egypt.	1956
Israel wars with Egypt, Syria, Iraq, and Jordan.	1967
The Yom Kippur War.	1973
Egypt and Israel sign the Camp David Accords after peace negotiations.	1978
Israel invades Lebanon.	1982
First-ever peace talks between Israel and Jordan, Lebanon, Syria, Saudi Arabia, and the Palestinians are held in Madrid, Spain.	1991
Jordan's King Hussein and Israel's Prime Minister Yitzhak Rabin sign peace accord.	1994
Prime Minister Rabin is assassinated.	1995
Peace talks continue.	1997

World History

1492	Columbus arrives in North America.
1500s	The Reformation leads to the birth of Protestantism.
1776	The Declaration of Independence is signed.
1789	The French Revolution begins.
1865	The American Civil War ends.
1914	World War I breaks out.
1917	The Bolshevik Revolution brings Communism to Russia.
1929	Worldwide economic depression begins.
1939	World War II begins, following the German invasion of Poland.
1957	The Vietnam War starts.
1989	The Berlin Wall is torn down, as Communism crumbles in Eastern Europe.
1996	Bill Clinton re-elected U.S. president.

Fast Facts

Official name: State of Israel

Capital: Jerusalem

Official languages: Hebrew and Arabic

Jerusalem

Flag of Israel

A Palestinian refugee

Yeshiva students

Official religions: Judaism, 81%; Islam, 15%

National anthem: *Hatikvah* ("The Hope")

Founding date: May 14, 1948

Founder: David Ben-Gurion, first prime minister

Government: Republic

Chief of state: President

Head of government: Prime minister

Area: 8,474 square miles (21,946 sq km)

Coordinates of geographic center: 31° 30' N, 34° 45' E

Bordering countries: Lebanon, Syria, Jordan, and Egypt

Highest elevation: Mount Meron (*Har Meron*), 3,963 feet (1,208 m)

Lowest elevation: Dead Sea, 1,312 feet (400 m) below sea level

Average temperatures: January: 73°F (23°C)
August: 80°F (27°C)

Average annual rainfall: 28 inches (71 cm) in the north and 8 inches (20 cm) in the south

National population (1998): 5,987,000

Population of largest cities (1996):

Jerusalem (including East Jerusalem)	602,100
Tel Aviv-Jaffa	353,100
Haifa	255,300
Rishon Le-Ziyyon	171,100
Holon	163,900
Petah Tikwa	154,500
Beersheba (1992)	128,400

The fortress of Masada

Currency

Famous landmarks: Many shrines in Israel have special meaning to the world's major religions. Jerusalem is home to the Dome of the Rock (Muslim), Church of the Holy Sepulchre (Christian), and the Western Wall (Jewish). Secular landmarks include the modern lines of the Israeli Supreme Court and the Israel Museum in Jerusalem, the Golda Meir Center for the Performing Arts in Tel Aviv, and the bustling port of Haifa. Geographical landmarks include the Dead Sea, the Jordan River, the Judean and Negev Deserts, and the extensive beaches along the country's coast.

Industry: Israel's major industries include food processing, diamond cutting and polishing, manufacturing of textiles, chemicals, metal products, and military equipment. The mining of potash is also important, as is tourism.

Currency: Israel's official currency is the new Israeli shekel (NIS). In 1999, U.S. $1 = 4.09 NIS.

Weights and measures: Metric system

Literacy rate: About 100%

Common Hebrew words and phrases:

Shalom	Hello *or* Good-bye
Boker tov	Good morning
Erev tov	Good evening
Ken	Yes
Lo	No
Toda	Thank you
Bevakasha	Please *or* You're welcome

The Church of the Holy Sepulchre

Peace talks

Common Arabic words and phrases:

Salaam aleikum	Hello (formal)
Marhaba	Hello (informal)
Aleikum as-salaam	(response to "Hello")
Sabah al-kheir	Good morning
Masa' al-kheir	Good evening
Aiwa	Yes
La	No
Shukran	Thank you
Min fadlak	Please (to a man)
Min fadlik	Please (to a woman)

Famous Israelis:

Shmuel Yosef Agnon (1888–1970)
Author

Hayim Nahman Bialik (1873–1934)
Poet

Menachem Begin (1913–1992)
Prime minister and Nobel Prize–winner

David Ben-Gurion (1886–1973)
Prime minister

Golda Meir (1898–1978)
Prime minister

Benjamin Netanyahu (1949–)
Prime minister

Yitzhak Perlman (1945–)
Musician

Yitzhak Rabin (1922–1995)
Prime minister and Nobel Prize–winner

Ido Tadmor (1964–)
Dancer

To Find Out More

Nonfiction

▶ Beilin, Yossi. *Israel: A Concise Political History, 1992*. New York: St. Martin's Press, 1993.

▶ Bright, John. *A History of Israel*. Philadelphia: Westminster Press, 1972.

▶ Cahill, Mary Jane. *Israel*. Broomall, Pa.: Chelsea House, 1997.

▶ Diqs, Isaak. *A Bedouin Boyhood*. New York: Universe Books, 1967.

▶ Friedmahn, Thomas L. *From Beirut to Jerusalem*. New York: Anchor Books, 1995.

▶ Harris, Nathaniel. *Israel and the Arab Nations in Conflict*. Chatham, N.J.: Raintree/Steck Vaughn, 1998.

▶ Long, Cathryn J. *The Middle East in Search of Peace*. Brookfield, Conn.: Millbrook, 1996.

▶ Roberts, Samuel J. *Party and Policy in Israel: The Battle between Hawks and Doves*. Boulder: Westview Press, 1990.

▶ Sacher, Howard M. *A History of Israel: From the Rise of Zionism to Our Time*. New York: Alfred A. Knopf, 1985.

▶ Schroeter, Daniel J. *Israel: An Illustrated History*. New York: Oxford University Press, 1998.

▶ Waldman, Neil. *Masada*. New York: Morrow Junior, 1998.

The Holocaust

▶ Boas, Jacob, ed. *We Are Witnesses: Five Diaries of Teenagers Who Died in the Holocaust*. New York: Henry Holt, 1995.

► Jackson, Livia Bitton. *I Have Lived a Thousand Years*. New York: Simon & Schuster, 1997.

► Rossell, Seymour. *The Holocaust: The World and the Jews, 1933–1945*. West Orange, N.J.: Behrman House, 1992.

Biography

► Adler, David A. *Our Golda: The Story of Golda Meir*. New York: Viking, 1986.

► Biracree, Tom. *Chaim Weizmann: President of Israel*. Broomall, Pa.: Chelsea House, 1988.

► Gurko, Miriam. *Theodore Herzel: The Road to Israel*. Philadelphia: Jewish Publication Society, 1989.

Fiction

► Ashabrenner, Brent K. *Gavriel and Jemal, Two Boys of Jerusalem*. New York: Dodd, Mead, 1984.

Websites

► **CIA World Factbook**
http://www.odci.gov/cia/publications/factbook/country-frame.html
Detailed statistical information on Israel, the Gaza Strip, and the West Bank from the U.S. government

► **Infotour**
http://www.infotour.co.il
Information on the people, land, and tourist sites of Israel from the Ministry of Tourism of Israel

Organizations and Embassies

► Embassy of Israel
3514 International Drive NW
Washington, DC 20008
(202) 364-5500

► Israel Tourism Information Center
Israel Ministry of Tourism
800 Second Avenue
16th Floor
New York, NY 10017
(888) 77-ISRAEL *or*
(212) 499-5640

Index

Page numbers in *italics* indicate illustrations.

A

Abu–Shakra, Asim, 111, *111*
academic schools, 80
agama lizards, 25, *25*
Agnon, Shmuel Yosef, 72, 133
agriculture, 8, 9, 12, *62*, 63–64, *63*,
    64, 66
    Baron Edmond de Rothschild
        and, 37
    irrigation, 67
    kibbutzim (communal farms),
        38–39, *39*
    livestock, 29, *29*
    map, *70*
    moshav (agricultural
        settlement), 39
    schools, 80
Ahsse, Sharon, 107
aliyah (immigration to Israel), 91
Almagor, Gila, 111
alpacas, 67, *67*
animal life, 24–26, *24*
    alpacas, 67, *67*
    bird species, 28, *28*
    brown bear, 28
    camels, 9, 30, *30*
    Canaan dogs, 29–30, *29*
    Ein Gedi Nature Reserve, 124
    fallow deer, 26
    fennec fox, 27, *27*
    ibex, *24*, 25
    livestock, 29, *29*
    military and, 26
    mountain gazelle, 25
    ostriches, 26, *26*
    Somali wild asses, 26
    Tisch Family Biblical Zoo and
        Zoological Gardens, 27–28
    white oryx, 26
Arab Hashemite Kingdom of
    TransJordan, 42
Arab Theater, 111
Arabic language, 84, 86
Arad, Yael, 117, *117*
Arafat, Yasser, 48, *48*, 58
Aramaic language, 84
archaeology, 33–34, *33*
    map, 34
Ariel (literary magazine), 107
art, 20, 112, *112*, 119, 123

B

Baha'i religion, 101–102, *101*
Balfour Declaration, 40, 42
bar mitzvahs, 95
Barenboim, Daniel, 107
Basic Laws, 54
Basilica of the Nativity, 35
bat mitzvahs, 95
Beckermann, Ruth, 111
Bedouins, 9, 28–29
Beersheba, 20, 28–29
    Ben-Gurion University of
        the Negev, 20
    climate of, 20
    population of, 20
Begin, Menachem, 46–47, *47*, 133
Ben-Gurion University of
    the Negev, 20
Ben-Gurion Airport, 75
Ben-Gurion, David, 51, *51*, 54, 133
Ben-Yehuda, Eliezer, 37
Ben-Zvi, Yitzhak, 72
Bethlehem, 13, *13*
Bialik, Hayim Nahman, 106, 133
bird species, 28, *28*
Black Hebrews, 103
borders, 15–17
Brody, Tal, 116
brown bears, 28

C

cable TV, 74
camels, 9, 30, *30*
Canaan dogs, 29–30, *29*
Canada Centre, 12–13
Carter, Jimmy, 46, *47*
Catholicism, 102, *102*
cell phones, 74, *74*
Chagall, Marc, 124
Chait, Galit, 116
cholent (stew), 121, *121*
Christianity, 13, *13*, 35, 102
Church of the Holy Sepulchre,
    35, *35*, 103
cities
    Beersheba, 20, 28–29
    Bethlehem, 13, *13*
    Eilat, *14*, 20, 45, 108

Haifa, 18, 20, 75
Jaffa, 76, 83–84
Jericho, 17, 33, *33*
Jerusalem, 9, 15, 18, *19*, 27, *32*, 34, 40, 89, 108
Tel Aviv, 11–12, *11*, 18–20, *20*
Zefat, 20
climate, 24
    Beersheba, 20
    Eilat, 20
    Haifa, 20
    Jordan River and, 23
    plant life and, 31
    Tel Aviv, 20
    Zefat, 20
Clinton, Bill, 48–49, *48*
clothing, 92
coastline, 15, 17
Committee of the Hebrew Language, 106
communications, 74–75
    cell phones, 74, *74*
    Israel Broadcasting Authority, 98
currency (sheqalim), 72, *72*

D
dance, *104*, 109–111
Dayan, Moshe, *56*
Dead Sea, 19, 21–22, *21*
    as a mining area, 70, *71*
    as a resort area, 69–70, *69*
Dead Sea Scrolls, 22, *22*
Declaration of Independence, 51–54
Degania kibbutz, *39*
desalination process, 69
Diaspora, 35
Dome of the Rock, 9, *9*, 99, *99*
dromedary (one-humped camel), 30
Druze culture, 100–101

E
economy, 23

currency (sheqalim), 72, *72*
foreign aid, 67
Golan Heights and, 70
international trade, 65, 70
irrigation, 68, *68*
Jerusalem Mall, 125, *125*
technology industries, 73
Tel Aviv Stock Exchange, 72, *73*
tourism, 62
unemployment rate, 72
winemaking industry, 65
education
    Ben Gurion University of the Negev, 20
    governmental grants for, 94
    Hebrew University, 42
    Ministry of Culture and Education, 81
    religion and, 80
    universities, 81, *81*
    yeshivot (religious schools), 93
Egypt, attack on Israel, 46
Eilat, *14*, 20, 45
    climate of, 20
    population of, 20
    Red Sea Jazz Festival, 108
Ein Gedi Nature Reserve, 24, 124
Ein Hod (artists village), 112–113, *112*
Ein Kerem, 120–121, *120*, 123
El Al airline, 75
elections, 56, *57*
environmental protection, 25
Epher, Reuven, 27
Ethiopian Jews, 77, *77*
Euro Music competition, 107
Eve's Daughters (klezmer band), 109
Eyal, Amalia, 111

F
fallow deer, 26
Famous people, 133. *See also* people.
Feast of Sukkot, 84, 96

Feld dance troupe, *109*
fennec fox, 27, *27*
ferry services, 75
film industry, 111
foods
    camel milk, 30
    cholent (stew), 121, *121*
    gazoz (fruit-flavored drink), 121
    religion and, 121
    zalabi, 127
forest-reclamation projects, 30, *31*
Fridman, Gal, 117
fruits, 65, 127

G
Galilee, 8
Gaon, Yehoram, 105
Gaza Strip, 16–18, *17*, 47
gazoz (fruit-flavored drink), 121
geography, 15, 24
geopolitical map, 10
Golan Heights, 12, 15, 65–66, *65*, *66*, 70
Golda Meir Center for the Performing Arts, 20, 109
government, 15, 17, 53, 54. *See also* local government.
    cabinet, 57
    educational grants, 94
    Knesset (parliament), 53–54, *54*, 56
    political party, 57
    presidential elections, 56, *57*
    prime minister, 57
    religion and, 89–91
    United States Embassy, 11–12
Greek Orthodox Church, 88, 102
Gross, Yaakov, 111
Grotto of the Nativity, 13
Gulf of Aqaba, *14*

H
Hadassah Hospital, 123–124

Hai-Bar National Biblical Wildlife
	Reserve, 26
Haifa, 18, 20, 75
	Baha'i Shrine, 101, *101*
	climate of, 20
	population of, 20
Haifa Repertory Theater, 111
halakah (Jewish religious law), 61
Hapoel Gailil Elyon (basketball
	team), 115
Hapoel Jerusalem (soccer team), 122
haredim (Orthodox Jews), 93
Hatikvah (national anthem), 53
Hebrew language, 37, 77, 84, 86, 106
Hebrew Scouts, 126, *126*
Hebrew University, 42
Hecht Synagogue, 89
Herzl, Theodor, 38, *38*, 52
Histadrut (General Federation
	of Labor), 61
Hitler, Adolf, 42
holidays, 124
Holocaust, 50
	Jewish Brigade and, 43
	Yad Vashem (Museum of the
		Holocaust), 82–83, *82*
Holy Land, map of, 36
hora (folk dance), 111
housing, 63
Hoveve-Zion. *See* Lovers of Zion.
Hula Nature Reserve, 26
Hussein, king of Jordan, 59
Hyams, Phillip, 106

I

ibex (animal), *24*, 25
ice hockey, 13
Ilana Goor Museum and Gallery, 112
Imber, Naphtali Herz, 53
immigration, 77–78, 91
	restrictions, 42–43
Indian Jews, 77–78, *78*

International Birdwatching Center, 28
international trade, 65, 70
irrigation, 67–68, *68*
Isaacson, David, 112
Islamic religion
	Koran (Muslim holy book), 61, 96
	Mecca (holy city), 98
	mosques, 9, 98
	muezzin (Muslim crier), 13
	Muhammad, 97
	Muslims, 96, 98
	Ramadan (month of fasting),
		97, 124
Israel Ballet Company, 109
Israel Broadcasting Authority, 74, 98
Israel Communications
	Corporation, 74
Israel Defense Forces, 74
Israel Museum, 112, *118*, 125
Israel Philharmonic Orchestra,
	105, 107
Israeli Basketball League, 115
Israely, Shimon, 111
Ivgi, Uri, 110

J

Jaffa, 11, *11*, 76, 83–84
Jericho, 17, 33, *33*, 47
Jerusalem, 9, 15, 18, *19*, 34, 40, 85, 123
	Church of the Holy Sepulchre, 103
	Designer Quarter, 112
	Dome of the Rock, 9, *9*, 99, *99*
	Ein Kerem, 120–121, *120*, 123
	Hecht Synagogue, 89
	Israel Museum, 112
	Leonard Bernstein International
		Music Competition, 108
	map of, *55*
	Mea Shearim (haredi
		community), 93
	Old City, *122*, 127
	Ottoman Turks capture of, 36

Tisch Family Biblical Zoo and
	Zoological Gardens, 27–28
Tower of David Citadel, *32*, 41
Tower of David Museum, 108
Jerusalem Artists' House, 119
Jerusalem Film Center, 111
Jerusalem Film Festival, 111
Jerusalem Mall, 125, *125*
Jerusalem Symphony Orchestra, 108
Jewish Agency for Palestine, 42, 61
Jewish Brigade, 43
Jewish Consciousness Program, 82
Jewish National Fund, 30–31
Jewish culture, 32, 34, 35, 36, 51
	Ethiopian Jews, 77, *77*
	haredim (Orthodox Jews), 93
	Holocaust, 43, 50
	immigrants, 77
	Indian Jews, 77–78, *78*
	Muslims and, 98
	violence against, 42
jihad (holy war), 59
Jordan
	as Arab Hashemite Kingdom
		of TransJordan, 42
	treaty with Israel, 48
Jordan Rift Valley, 22
Jordan River, 12, *18*, 19, 22–23, *23*,
	67, *113*. *See also* West Bank.
Judaica, 112
Judaism, 9
	bar mitzvahs, 95, 109
	bat mitzvahs, 95, 109
	kosher laws, 121
	rabbis (teachers of Jewish law), 96
	Rosh Hashanah (Jewish New
		Year), 95–96
	tallith (fringed shawl), 92
	Talmud (religious text), 93
	tefillin (black Torah boxes), 92–93
	Torah (Jewish law), 93, 94
	yarmulke (cap), 92

Judean language, 84
judicial branch (of government), 59–61
   halakah (Jewish religious law), 61
   image of justice, 60

K

kabala (Jewish mysticism), 20
Karaites, 103
Karam stock index, 72
Karmi, Ram, 60
kibbutzim (communal farms), 36, 38, 39, *39*, 110
King Hussein Bridge, *126*
kinot (dirges), 95
klezmer instrumental music, 109
Klieger, Noah, 116
Knesset (parliament), 53–54, *54*, 56
Koran (Muslim holy book), 61, 96

L

Labor Party, 57
languages, 85
   Arabic, 84, 86
   Aramaic, 84
   Committee of the Hebrew Language, 106
   Hebrew, 37, 77, 84, 86, 106
   Judean, 84
   Russian, 86
   Yiddish, 85–86
Law of Return, 91
Lawrence of Arabia (T. E. Lawrence), 40, *40*
Leaf, Brad, 115
League of Nations, 41
Lebanon
   Israeli invasion of, 47
   Israeli occupation of, 18
Leonard Bernstein International Music Competition, 108
Likud (Liberal) Party, 57

literature, 85, 105–107
livestock, 29, *29*, 66, *66*
local government, 61
Lot's Wife (passenger ship), 21–22
Lovers of Zion, 38

M

Maccabi Tel Aviv (basketball team), 115–116, *115*
Magen David. *See* Shield of David.
Makhtesh Ramon. *See* Ramon Crater.
Mann Auditorium, 107
manufacturing, 64, *71*
maps
   agricultural, *70*
   archaeological, *34*
   geopolitical, *10*
   Holy Land, *36*
   Jerusalem, *55*
   natural resources, *70*
   Old City (Jerusalem), *55*
   population density, *79*
   topographical, *16*
   United Nations (UN) partition, *44*
Masada fortress, *34*, 35, 123, *123*
Mashalah, Salman, 85, 107
Mea Shearim (haredi community), 93
Mecca (Islamic holy city), 98
Mediterranean Sea, 11, 14–15, *15*
mehozot (administrative districts), 61
Meir, Golda, 56, 57, 133
Melamede, Ada Karmi, 60
Menin, Olga, 117
menorah (candelabrum), 52, *52*
Michaeli, Rivka, 111–112
military, 36, 59, 65, 74, 86, 95, 101
   animal life and, 26
   Jewish Brigade, 43
   women in, 86–87, *87*
   yeshiva student exemption from, 93
minaret (mosque tower), 97
mining, 64, 70, *71*

Ministry of Culture and Education, 81
Ministry of Environment, 25
Ministry of Religious Affairs, 98
Mishtanim stock index, 72
moshav (agricultural settlement), 39
mosques, 9, 97–98
   minaret (tower), 97
mountain gazelle, 25
muezzins (Muslim criers), 13, 97
Museum of Contemporary Art, 112
Museum of the Holocaust, 82–83, *82*
music, 107–109
   Hatikvah (national anthem), 53
   Israel Philharmonic Orchestra, *105*, 107
Muslims, 96, 98

N

Nahrin, Ohad, 110
Nahum Goldmann Museum of the Jewish Diaspora, 84
National Day, 124
national flag, 50, 52, *52*
natural resources
   Dead Sea and, 22
   map of, *70*
Nature Reserve Authority, 25–26
Negev Center for Regional Development, 23, 25
Negev Desert, 19, 20–21, 26, 28
Neot Kedumim landscape reserve, 31
Netanyahu, Benjamin, 58, *59*, 133
New Israel Fund, 61
newspapers, 75

O

Old City (Jerusalem), 55, 127
Olympic Games, 46, 116, *117*
ostriches, 26, *26*
Ottoman Turks
   capture of Jerusalem, 36
   Lawrence of Arabia and, 40

P

Pablo Casals Cello Competition, 108
Palestine, 33, 36, 40–41, *43*, 44, 50
    Balfour Declaration, 40
    Muslim extremists, 49
    Roman Empire and, 34
Palestine Liberation Organization, 17
Palestinian refugees, 17, *17*
Palestinians, 18
Peace Now Organization, 61
people, *63, 76, 77, 80, 81, 83,*
    93, 118. See also Famous people.
    Bedouins, 9, 28–29
    Druze, 100–101
    immigration restrictions, 42–43
    Israelites, 34
    Jews, 32, 34–36, 42, *43*, 51
    Karaites, 103
    Muslims, 96, 98
    Palestinians, 17–18
    Philistines, 33
    Samaritans, 103
Peres, Shimon, *58*
Perlman, Yitzhak, 107, *107*, 133
Phil tobacco factory, 73
Philistia, 33
Philistines, 33
Phillipe, Sam, 112
plant life, 9, 23–25, *31*
    climate and, 31
    forest-reclamation projects, 30, *31*
    Neot Kedumim landscape
        reserve, 31
    sabras (prickly pear cactus), 79, *79*
    Tu B'shvat (New Year of Trees), 31
    wildflowers, 25
political parties
    Labor Party, 57
    Likud (Liberal) Party, 57
    religion and, 91
population, 76, 79

Beersheba, 20
density map, *79*
Eilat, 20
Haifa, 20
Tel Aviv, 20
Zefat, 20
Postal Authority, 74
potash mining, 70, *71*
prime minister, 57

R

rabbis (teachers of Jewish law), 96
Rabin, Yitzhak, 58, *58*, 133
    assassination of, 58
    Israeli treaty with Jordan and,
        48, *48*
radio, 74
railways, 75
Ramadan (Islamic month of fasting),
    97–98, 124
Ramon Crater, 19, 21
rappelling (sport), *114*
rebbes. *See* rabbis.
Red Sea Jazz Festival, 108
religion, 13, *13*, 88, 95, 98, 121
    Baha'i, 101–102
    Basilica of the Nativity, 35
    Black Hebrews, 103
    Catholicism, 102, *102*
    Christianity, 35, 102
    Church of the Holy Sepulchre,
        35, *35*, 103
    Dead Sea Scrolls, 22, *22*
    education and, 80
    foods and, 121
    government and, 89–91
    Greek Orthodox Church, 88, 102
    halakah (Jewish religious law), 61
    image of justice, 60
    Islamic, 96
    jihad (holy war), 59

Jordan River, 12
Judaism, 9
kabala (Jewish mysticism), 20
Karaites, 103
muezzin (Muslim crier), 13
    political parties and, 91
    Roman Catholic Church of
        All Nations, 90
    Samaritans, 103
    Sea of Galilee, 23
    Uniate religious sect, 102
    Western Wall, 9, *11*, 93,
        94–95, *95*
reptilian life, 25, *25*
roadways, 75, *126*
rock and roll music, 108–109
Roman Catholic Church of
    All Nations, 90
Roman Empire, Palestine and, 34
Rosenblum, Jonathan, 78
Rosh Hashanah (Jewish New Year),
    95–96
de Rothschild, Baron Edmond, 37, *37*
rugby, 114
Russian language, 86

S

sabras (prickly pear cactus), 79, *79*
el-Sadat, Anwar, 46, *47*
Safrai gallery, 119
Sakanovsky, Sergei, 116
Samaritans, 103
Samuel, Sir Herbert, 41, *41*
Scharf, Sholmo, 114
Sea of Galilee, 12, *12*, 19, 23, 67, 88
Segal, Zelig, 112
Sharet, Moshe, 72
sherut taxis, 75
Shield of David, 52, *52*
Shmerkin, Misha, 116–117
Sinai Desert, 44

"Six-Day War," 45, *45*, 66, 94–95
Smadja, Oren, 117
soccer, 95, *114*, 122
Solomon's Pools, 12
Somali wild asses, 26
sports, 113–117
    basketball, 115
    Hapoel Jerusalem (soccer
        team), 122
    ice hockey, 13
    Olympic Games, 46
    rappelling, *114*
    rugby, 114
    soccer, 95, 122
    Teddy Kollek soccer stadium, 125
Spring of the Virgin, 120
State of Israel
    flag of, 52, *52*
    independence ceremony, 52–53
Suez Canal, 44–45
Supreme Court, 59–60, *60*
Suzanne Dellal Centre for Dance
    and Theatre, 110
Suzanne Dellal International Dance
    Competition, 110
Syria
    attack on Israel, 46
    Israeli peace talks with, 48

T

Tadmor, Ido, 110, *110*, 133
tallith (fringed shawl), 92
Talmud (religious text), 93
technology industries, 73
Teddy Kollek soccer stadium, 125
tefillin (black Torah boxes), 92–93
Tel Aviv, 11–12, *11*, 18–20, *20*
    climate of, 20
    Golda Meir Center for the
        Performing Arts, 20
    Mann Auditorium, 107

Museum of Contemporary
    Art, 112
    nightclubs in, 109
    Suzanne Dellal International
        Dance Competition, 110
    University of Tel Aviv, 84
Tel Aviv Museum of Art, 20
Tel Aviv Stock Exchange, 72, *73*
television, 74
terrorism, 46, 49, *49*, 100
Tisch Family Biblical Zoo and
    Zoological Gardens, 27–28
topographical map, *16*
Torah (Jewish law), 93, 94
tourism, 62, 69–70, *69*, 121, 124
Tower of David Citadel, *32*, 41
Tower of David Museum, 108
Transition Law, 53–54
transportation, 75, *123*
Truman, Harry S., 43
Tu B'shvat (New Year of Trees), 31
Twelve Tribes of Israel, 33

U

unemployment rate, 72
Uniate religious sect, 102
United Nations (UN), 13
    intervention by, 44–45, 47
    partition map, *44*
United States Embassy, 11–12
University of Tel Aviv, 84

V

Valley Region, 19
vocational schools, 80

W

"Wailing Wall." *See* Western Wall.
water supply, 67, 69
Weizman Institute of Science, 73
Weizmann, Chaim, *44*

West Bank, 16–18, *18*, 47. *See also*
    Jordan River.
Western Wall, 9, *11*, 93, 94–95, *95*
white oryx, 26
whitewater rafting, 113, *113*
wildflowers, 25
wildlife. *See* animal life; plant life;
    reptilian life.
wine-making industry, 65
women, military service and,
    86–87, *87*
World Cup tournament, *114*
World Maccabiah Games, 116
World War I, 38, 40–41
World War II, 20, 43, 50, 77
World Zionist Organization, 61
Writers' Association, 106
Wye River Memorandum, 49

Y

Yad Vashem. *See* Museum of
    the Holocaust.
Yam Hamelah. *See* Dead Sea.
Yam Kinneret. *See* Sea of Galilee.
Yarkon Park, 107
yarmulke (cap), 92
yeshivot (religious schools), 80, 93
    yeshiva students, 94
Yiddish language, 85–86
Yom Kippur (Day of Atonement), 96

Z

zalabi (food), 127
Zefat, 20
    climate of, 20
    population of, 20
Zionist Movement, 38, 42
    flag of, 52, *52*
    State of Israel and, 51–52
Zommer, Raya, 113

Meet the Authors

M

ARTIN HINTZ has written several books in the Enchantment of the World series, including *The Bahamas*, *Poland*, *Haiti*, and *The Netherlands*. Regular visits to the library and the Internet were valuable in preparing this manuscript. Martin also visited Israel several times. He spent time with artists, politicians, businesspeople, ordinary folks in the markets, and other Israelis who talked about their marvelous nation. He traveled through the desert, listened to opera, visited art galleries, meandered through the Old City of Jerusalem, and received a mud pack at a Dead Sea resort.

Martin is a member of the Society of American Travel Writers and other professional journalist organizations. In addition to almost sixty books, he has written hundreds of magazine and newspaper articles. Martin has a master's degree in journalism from Northwestern University.

STEPHEN HINTZ has shared writing jobs with his father for several publishers, including Children's Press. He coauthored *North Carolina* in the America the Beautiful series and *The Bahamas* in the Enchantment of the World series. To prepare for this book, Steve also visited Israel and Jordan. He rafted along the Jordan River, rode camels, climbed cliffs, ate with desert Bedouins, and sailed on the Dead Sea. He is a 1996 graduate of the University of Wisconsin–Milwaukee with a degree in sociology and African-American studies.

Photo Credits

956.94   Hintz, Martin.
Hin   Israel
c.3

PERMA-BOUND®

DATE DUE			